Jet Warplanes
THE TWENTY-FIRST CENTURY

Jet Warplanes
THE TWENTY-FIRST CENTURY

Michael J. H. Taylor

BISON BOOKS

Published by
Bison Books Ltd.
176 Old Brompton Road,
London, SW 5
England.

ISBN 0 86124 315 3

Printed in Hong Kong

Reprinted 1988

Page 1: Concept for an advanced tactical fighter for operation in the 21st century.

Pages 4-5: A single-seat combat version of the BAe Hawk trainer flew for the first time in 1986 as the Hawk Series 200.

Pages 2-3: The Grumman Intruder will still be the US Navy's standard low-level, all-weather, and day and night deep strike attacker through the 1990s.

CONTENTS

INTRODUCTION

Jet Warplanes — the 21st Century is not merely a book of futuristic concepts and designs illustrated with artist's impressions of strangely shaped warplanes; if it were it would be better entitled 'Futuristic Fighters and Bombers'. The book in fact presents the aircraft likely to be flying at the start of the 21st century. Many fighters and bombers mentioned and illustrated are certainly futuristic, but mingled with these are warplanes currently in production or due for deployment in the 1990s, all of which will be seen at the turn of the century.

By far the greater part of the information given in the text is based on known facts received from many sources, with as little speculation injected as possible. Though some of the conclusions may, with the passage of time, prove to be unfounded, all the theories, projects and programs detailed are known to be under serious consideration or in some stage of fulfilment; concepts so speculative as to be unworthy of the title have been left aside.

The first chapter of the book may at first glance appear to have little to do with fighters and bombers, though it mentions space warfare and space planes among other subjects. It is, however, essential for the reader to understand something of the force multipliers and defense systems which assist or hinder aircraft undertaking wartime missions, and designers of fighters and bombers have to reckon with.

The author would like to thank the many individuals, organizations and companies whose assistance has greatly benefited this book, especially Bill Gunston, British Aerospace, Grumman Aerospace, Lockheed-California and GEC Avionics.

Left: Artist's conception of a triple-nozzle vectored-thrust supersonic fighter for the 1990s and beyond, suited to replace conventional fighters on carrier decks.

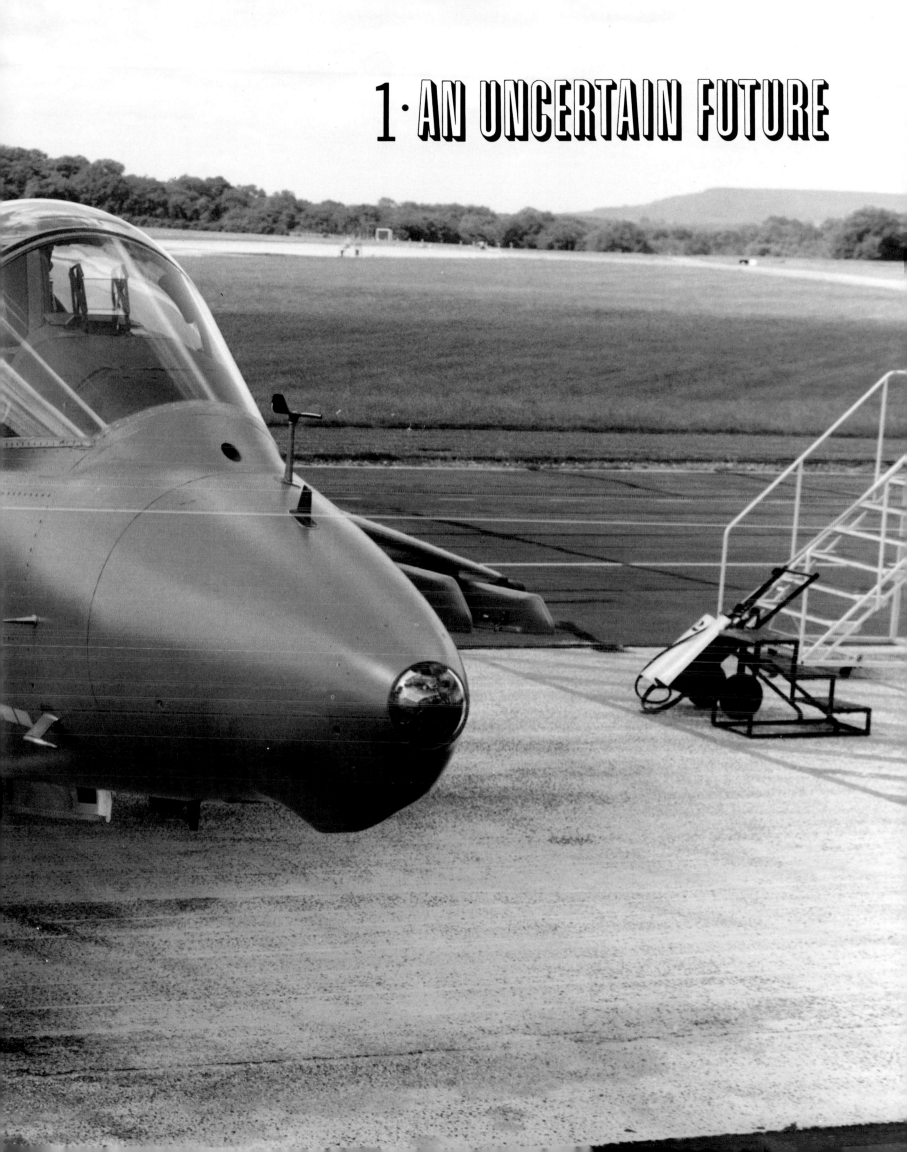

Whatever the outcome of superpower summits over the next decade and a half, new technologies and systems in the research and development stages in the 1980s will greatly affect military aviation by AD 2000. These take many forms, ranging from the configurations, avionics and power plants of future combat aircraft, and the materials used in their construction, to new offensive and defensive weapons, detection and tracking systems, force multipliers and so on.

The greatest uncertainty at present seems to be about space and what will be allowed in terms of space weapons. The outcome of space treaties will affect developments in many possible scenarios, including the deployment of manned aircraft for certain tasks. Spy and missile launch detection satellites already use space, the latter providing perhaps a 30-minute warning of an incoming intercontinental ballistic missile (ICBM) strike. Satellites therefore are high-priority targets in time of war and both the USSR and the USA have developed anti-satellite systems. In the 1980s the Soviet Asat system comprised ground-launched satellites based at Tyuratam and armed with conventional warheads. The US system (following in about 1987) relies on two squadrons of McDonnell Douglas F-15 Eagle fighters based at Langley, Virginia, each carrying a missile with a Vought air-launched miniature vehicle. The ALMV has an infra-red terminal seeker and conventional war-

head which is set spinning at up to 20 revolutions per second for stabilization before separation from the missile, the complete weapon being fired while the fighter performs a zoom climb. However, this system is suited only to destroying enemy satellites at low orbital altitudes.

Space could also provide the home for the first generation Ballistic Missile Defense systems, the so-called 'star wars' systems, with Soviet and US research arguably providing an initial operational capability just after the turn of the century. The BMD systems will inevitably be more technologically demanding than, say, using space-based laser weapons for anti-satellite purposes, which could become a reality during the 1990s. Similar systems could also carry out anti-cruise missile roles and even the defense of 'friendly' aircraft, such as AWACS airborne early warning and control types. Another form of space weapon for anti-satellite purposes could be the kinetic energy system, relying on destruction by high-speed collision. More advanced than the laser systems would be space-deployed particle-beam weapons, perhaps offering an effective anti-satellite capability during the 1990s, initially intended to interfere with the satellite's sensors but with the advancement of the technology causing actual destruction.

Should future treaties ban these weapons from space (even though BMD systems are said to be defensive), lasers and particle-beam systems could

Previous pages: Harrier II showing its large unshielded engine fan, but nonetheless an essential fighting aircraft for the 1990s and beyond.

Below: Resembling the Mach 3+ SR-71A Blackbird strategic reconnaissance aircraft, this Lockheed-California conception of an Advanced Tactical Fighter (ATF) would adopt new advanced aluminum alloys for the airframe, though carbon graphite composites would be used for the inner parts of the airframe and titanium in areas where temperatures can reach 1000 degrees Fahrenheit.

Left: An artist's impression of the operational Soviet antisatellite interceptor in action.

Below: F-15 Eagle carrying the US Asat (antisatellite) missile on the center line station.

Above: A Boeing NKC-135 modified to act as an Airborne Laser Laboratory, flying near Kirtland Air Force Base, New Mexico. Any operational offensive airborne high-energy laser system would require a transport type 'motherplane' because of the electrical power required for the weapon, which would be 'fired' from a turret above the fuselage. The first air-to-air test, in mid-1981, failed to destroy the Sidewinder missile target but some success was later achieved, proving the difficulty of directing an intense beam of energy on a moving target over very long ranges.

Left: Soviet space shuttle transporting personnel and supplies to an advanced form of Salyut space station.

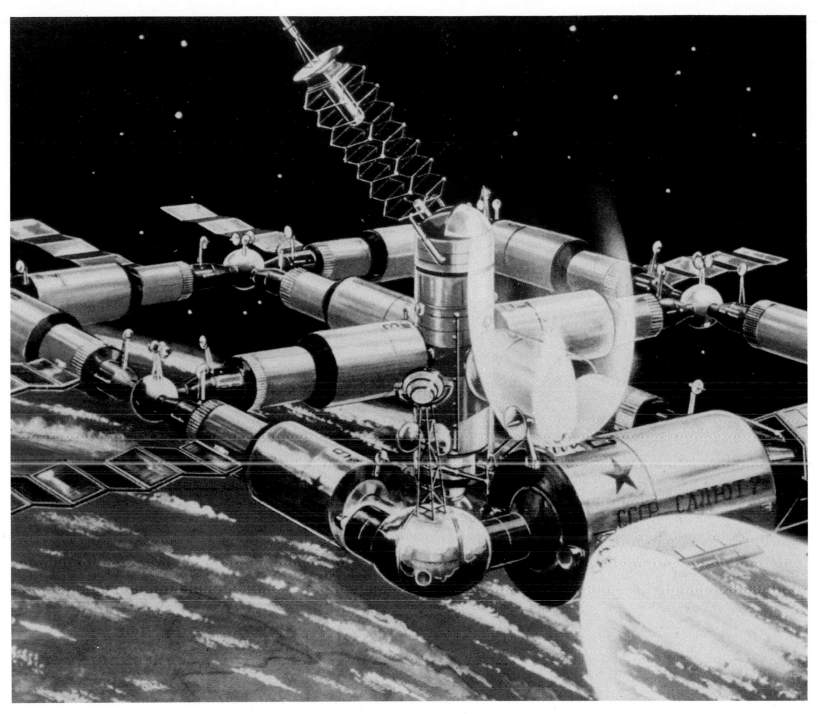

Above: Artist's conception of a Soviet manned space station of the future.

be ground deployed, joined later by radio-frequency weapons. Chemical, electric discharge and dynamic forms of laser are certainly under development, in addition to the other systems mentioned. It has been reported that the Soviet Union could be first to have operational ground-based anti-aircraft (and perhaps anti-satellite) laser systems, before the end of the 1980s. These would have two clear roles (as would any US or other nation's systems), namely to defend strategic locations from enemy attack in a similar way to the current complex of radar sites and missiles around Moscow, and to defend tactical forces from air attack. In either case, and with any operator, lasers would undoubtedly complement conventional anti-aircraft missile systems.

Tactical lasers would inevitably be smaller and less powerful than strategic high-energy weapons, but would nonetheless still be capable of destroying an aircraft at short range or at longer ranges could damage the attacking aircraft's avionic and optical systems and incapacitate the crew. Similar laser weapons could be installed on board ship or even be carried by aircraft.

The construction of large US and Soviet space stations could provide both high-priority targets in war and defensible command stations, though this is not to imply that either will be mostly military or totally non-military. Such stations could perhaps take over at least some of the command from Earth bases of intelligence, targeting, navigation, command, control and communications (C3), anti-satellite and other satellites that play vital roles in support of strategic and tactical ground, sea and air forces. As neither space station has yet been constructed, future treaties and cooperation (or lack of them) could alter greatly current plans for their use.

Both the US and USSR have reusable space shuttle vehicles and American expertise with this

Left: British Aerospace concept for an unmanned space platform to operate in conjunction with the US NASA manned space station. A permanent facility, it would have six berthing points along the 16-meter beam to carry up to six cargo pallets of 4000kg each, thereby offering users storage and launch facilities for cargoes, power, cooling, data services and orbital control in a contamination-free environment.

Opposite: US space shuttle orbiter with its cargo bay doors open. Orbiters are sometimes used to carry military payloads into space during closely guarded missions.

Below: Soviet subscale spacecraft, photographed by a RAAF Orion as it was hauled on deck.

type of spacecraft is already established. Alongside the large Soviet space shuttle a small spaceplane is thought to be under development, said by official Western sources to have the potential of giving the USSR the first ever reusable small manned spaceplane. Though such a craft could have several uses, including satellite inspection and other passive tasks, a manned and highly maneuverable spaceplane could be an outstanding satellite 'killer', also having major reconnaissance/intelligence capabilities. Aggressive uses for this or any future small spaceplane are of course only speculation, but its potential makes development of small spacefighters for superpower use a future certainty if not a current fact.

In 1982 and 1983 three Soviet subscale shuttle-like craft were launched into orbit under Cosmos serials, each later recovered from the Indian Ocean or Black Sea. The second recovery was photographed by a Royal Australian Air Force Lockheed Orion maritime patrol aircraft, allowing the subscale spaceplane to be identified.

The spaceplane weighed approximately 2000lb (907kg) and led US officials to believe it to be a scale test vehicle for an operational small spaceplane. An accompanying artist's impression of a Soviet spaceplane fighter on an anti-satellite mission was prepared for the US Department of Defense, and the clear similarity between the tested subscale vehicle and the drawn operational spaceplane indicates US belief that such a spaceplane is under development.

The operational small reusable spaceplane may only now be nearing reality, but the general con-

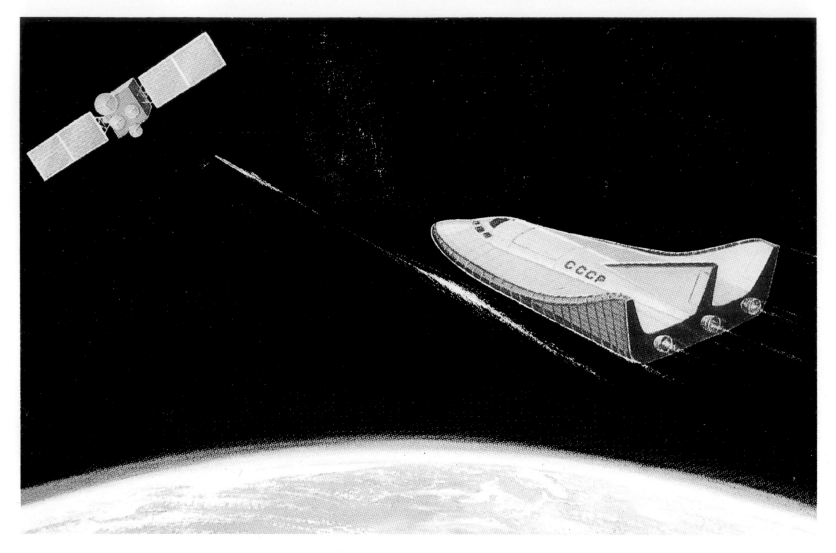

cept is not new. Back in the early 1960s a USAF/ NASA project covered the development of the X-20A Dyna-Soar, a delta-winged manned space glider intended to be boosted into space on the top of a Titan II rocket. It was expected to fly at speeds of more than 17,000mph (27,350km/h) and, once through the re-entry phase, was to glide back to base using aerodynamic control. A full-scale mock-up was displayed in Nevada in 1962 but in 1963 the Dyna-Soar program was canceled. The 'boost-glide' principle was tested, however, on a series of lifting-body re-entry research vehicles built by Northrop and Martin Marietta during the 1960s and 1970s, though these craft were released from airplanes and were not intended to leave the atmosphere. The data they provided were essential to the later development of the Space Shuttle Orbiter.

Leaving space, one of the major problems facing aircraft designers is that of remaining undetected long enough to complete a mission. This is particularly true for strategic bombers and smaller aircraft on penetration missions. One factor is the growing sophistication of radars. The main aim of satellites used for detection is to guard against ballistic missiles, and the same can be said of the new over-the-horizon radars that are now taking some of the burden from the satellites. These complement rather than replace the satellites, as the space sensors still offer greater precision for launch detection. OTH radars are also highly use-

ful in the detection of aircraft and cruise missiles, especially when an enemy attempts to spring a high-speed and/or low/high level attack.

Because this new form of radar can detect over the horizon, it greatly outclasses conventional radar and offers defenders longer to prepare a response. Several nations have been involved in OTH development, though the UK abandoned its lead in the field when it dismantled the antenna system based at Orfordness. However, it is believed the Australian Government bought the antenna system to use in its own OTH program under Project Jindalee. This nation appreciates its rather isolated defense position, surrounded by immense spans of ocean.

Two nations so far have operational OTH systems, naturally the USSR and the USA. Development has taken many years and has been brought to fruition only by the recent manufacture of the highly sophisticated processing equipment necessary to enable the extremely small return signals to be identified from the vast amounts of clutter. The two Soviet OTH radars diverge over the US mainland to concentrate on US ICBM sites. These radars can be seen as the final step in providing the Soviet Union with the most extensive radar early warning system in the world, suited to both missile and air defense, combining as they do with satellites, 11 ballistic missile warning detection and tracking radars (NATO name *Hen House*) at six sites around the borders of the nation, six

Above: US conception of a Soviet spacefighter on an antisatellite mission.

Right: Department of Defense illustration of the areas said to be covered by Soviet ballistic missile detection and tracking systems.

Far right: Artist's impression of a Soviet SA-X-12 air defense system, designed to counter high-performance aircraft.

Above: Not to be left out of the reusable spacecraft arena, France is leading a European effort to develop a vehicle somewhat smaller than the US/Soviet shuttles under the direction of CNES (Centre National d'Etudes Spatiales). Intended to carry 2-6 people and a cargo of five tonnes, it would be ideally suited to serve space stations. The Dassault-Breguet conception for *Hermes* is illustrated.

large phased-array radar sites either in use or under construction that form a surveillance arc from the Kola Peninsula in the northwest to the Caucasus in the southwest, the Moscow ABM radar/missile complex, and perhaps 7000 air surveillance radars that give an almost total cover over the USSR against aircraft and missiles flying at medium and high altitudes. Radar cover against low-flying aircraft and missiles is concentrated in the western sector of the USSR and at high-value locations elsewhere. Given an approximately 1250-strong strategic air defense interceptor force and an immense surface-to-air missile strength (with many thousands of antiaircraft missiles capable of ranges between 186 miles [300km] and just a few miles), the Soviet Union has provided the means to protect

itself and give an attacker the least possible chance of success.

The US over-the-horizon radar system is planned to comprise eight sectors, each giving a 60-degree scan over ranges of 500-1865 miles (800-3000km). The first three sectors became operational with the USAF in 1986-87, giving 180-degree coverage over the North Atlantic. This eastern seaboard group will be joined by a western group and eventually two southern sectors (all being operational before the 1990s), providing a ring around the US mainland when joining the DEW (distant early warning) radar chain that stretches across the North American continent from Alaska to Greenland. In addition there is BMEWS (Ballistic Missile Early Warning System),

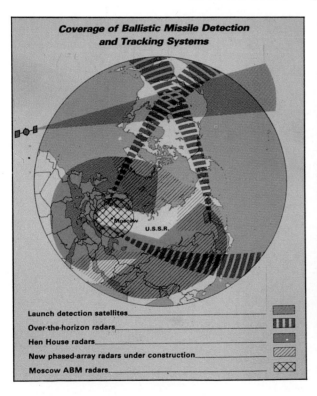

three very large radar sites located in Thule (Greenland), Clear (Alaska) and Fylingdales Moor (England), which complement three early warning satellites in the western and eastern hemispheres. Pave Paws phased array radars are used to give early warning of submarine-launched ballistic missile attack. All objects in space are detected, tracked and identified by the USAF's Spacetrack system and the US Navy's NAVSPASUR, both forming an element of NORAD (North American Air Defense Command) which undertakes co-ordination of the North American air defense surveillance and warning system. The Joint Surveillance System of air defense radar within NORAD is a US/Canadian operation.

Over-the-horizon radar operates in the high-frequency band, the conventional systems using transmissions bounced off the ionosphere. The backscatter return signals are picked up by a receiver and the processing systems sift among the clutter for the signal.

Another form of OTH radar is less understood, but promises to be a cheaper system and is likely to be well established by AD 2000. This surface wave system works on the principle that higher frequency radar transmissions appear to 'stick' to the surface of the water up to a height of perhaps 20-23ft (6-7m), thereby offering over-the-horizon capability but at the expense of range.

Weapons such as air-defense lasers and space-plane fighters, and highly sophisticated radar networks, all have to be taken into consideration when designing military aircraft for AD 2000 and beyond, the latter forcing the pace in the relatively new technology of 'low observability.' Improved infra-red sensors, particularly when fitted to homing missiles and satellites, may give even greater problems to designers, perhaps eventually forcing a new generation of warplanes to be built with engines lacking afterburners. Given that high-performance combat aircraft of the 1980s almost double their engine thrust with afterburning, this factor would be critical to design. More about this later.

The term 'force multiplier' is a convenient way of expressing under a single heading several forms of non-combat aircraft and systems that can greatly enhance the capability of armed warplanes. Force multipliers are used by all modern air forces and by AD 2000 they will have become even more essential. For an attacking group, force multipliers may take the form of electronic aircraft accompanying the attackers to confuse the enemy, pinpoint the target and jam enemy detection, tracking and weapon radars. For a defending force, especially when outnumbered, force multipliers can give the time to prepare the response, guide 'friendly' interceptors on to the attackers, confuse the attackers' electronic systems and counter the enemy's electronic countermeasures, and keep 'friendly' forces airborne on extended patrols.

Right: An ADVCAP (ADVanced CAPability) version of the Grumman EA-6 Prowler will still provide the US Navy with its ECM jamming capability in AD 2000.

Just one example of how force multipliers might work is when a large force of bombers attacks a superpower carrier battle group (CBG). Though an incredibly powerful sea force, a carrier battle group has restricted air power available to it. Even an aircraft carrier with, say, 86 aircraft on board may have only 24 dedicated fighters. However, with the assistance of an airborne early warning aircraft, these fighters can be given the time to press home an early and accurate interception. Two-way data links between AEW aircraft, the fighters and the control room on board ship can also provide better use of resources, the controller having an all-round picture of the situation and thereby making tactical judgments based on full information that is constantly updated. Electronic jamming aircraft can be launched to prevent the enemy force getting a radar fix on the CBG, and flight refueling tankers can keep the defending force airborne longer. Indeed, flight refueling tankers are very important in the 1980s but they are going to be essential by AD 2000 to service warplanes that may well be smaller and lighter.

Of the many forms force multipliers can take, probably the most essential is that of airborne early warning and control. The Falklands conflict of 1982 showed how vulnerable a task force operating a long way from home can be without AEW, the Royal Navy taking 'hits' that might have been avoided had an AEW aircraft been available to it. Further, V/STOL aircraft have high fuel consumption and the Sea Harriers could have been better employed had they been directed on to detected targets by a control plane. As a result of this experience, the Royal Navy took AEW Sea King helicopters on to its carriers.

Airborne early warning and control aircraft most often carry the radar antennae in a huge rotating 'saucer' carried above the aircraft's fuselage, though among large AEW aircraft is the RAF's Nimrod AEW Mk 3 which carries dual-frequency twisted cassegrain antennae in huge bulbous radomes at the nose and tail of the fuselage. The concept of the Nimrod installation is to remove the obscuration effects of the fuselage, as suffered by aircraft with above-fuselage antennae. Nimrod AEW will still be in use around AD 2000, as will the US Navy's carrier-based Hawkeye which will remain in production into the 1990s. The USAF's AWACS aircraft is the Boeing E-3 Sentry, which operates within NORAD and NATO and has been exported, but it is reasonable to expect a follow-up type to join the USAF before AD 2000 based on a more modern airframe than the Boeing 707. Certainly the Soviet Tupolev Tu-126 *Moss* will not survive until then, the superior Ilyushin Il-76 *Mainstay* (that began to filter into Soviet service in the mid 1980s) already offering much improved aircraft and cruise-missile detection over land and water.

Soviet *Kremlin* class nuclear-powered aircraft carriers that will become operational initially in the 1990s will also carry some form of airborne early warning and control aircraft. A new associated technology that will be used before AD 2000 is the conformal-array radar antenna, in which the

antenna follows the shape of the airframe. Tests began in 1986 of a US Navy Grumman E-2C Hawkeye with a conformal microprocessor controlled phased array antenna fitted to the wing leading edge, as part of an advanced anti-jamming electronic-countermeasures system.

AWACS types perform many functions and can even be used in civil roles. However, their main task is to provide long-range surveillance at all altitudes and of every form of air vehicle, whether manned or RPV/missile. Once detection has taken place it can track and possibly identify, while continuing the search for other targets. Its data storage and processing equipment provides real-time assessment of the enemy and the status of 'friendly' forces, and can direct 'friendly' forces on to the incoming enemy or help 'friendly' attackers elude enemy defenses. Such aircraft are particularly important to counter long-range cruise missiles, which can fly at very low altitudes indeed.

Above: One essential form of force multiplier is the in-flight refueling tanker, as seen here in the form of an RAF VC10 refueling a Tornado F.Mk 2 air defense interceptor.

Opposite: RAF Nimrod AEW Mk 3.

One form of AEW aircraft of the future could be the airship, though even this is not new as the US Navy operated non-rigid AEW airships from the later 1950s to 1961. The beauty of an airship is that the envelope makes an ideal radome for the surveillance radar, allowing antennae of greater size than can be carried easily by an airplane. Interestingly, it has been said that the British Government considered using an airship to carry surveillance radar during the Falklands conflict, but this came to nothing almost certainly because available airships were too small to carry the radar and still hold sufficient fuel on board for a long on-station endurance.

Long endurance is another factor making the airship an ideal force multiplier for the 1990s and the twenty-first century, counting such endurance in days or even weeks rather than hours. But there are other advantages. The envelopes of future military airships will be made of either fabric (for non-rigids) or advanced composite materials (for larger rigids), neither giving the telltale radar signatures for an enemy radar to pick up. However, its own radar and other parts of the airship would reflect a signal, but this can be reduced to a minimum by the adoption of radar absorbent material. Clearly, then, even airships will benefit from the use of modern materials and 'low observable' technology.

All early warning aircraft will of course be prime targets at the outbreak of any future war, and the airship's maximum speed of perhaps 100+ mph could be seen as a disadvantage against, say, five times that speed for large airplanes undertaking a similar role. But what the airship lacks in speed it can make up in cunning. Airships generally use fairly low-powered engines, often driving rotatable ducted propulsors to bestow VTOL capability. These engines are far less likely to be detected by infra-red sensors than the very large engines of an airplane. Further, the airship can switch off its engines to avoid IR detection and yet remain both airworthy and operational. In a form of 'hide and seek,' an airship could also attempt to avoid detection by flying into cloud, the helium gas in the envelope rapidly taking the ambient temperature. However, should the gas warm by the effects of the sun, it would become most visible to IR sensors.

By AD 2000 the AEW airship is likely to be a major force multiplier, while also undertaking such other military roles as maritime and exclusive economic zone (EEZ) patrol, antisubmarine patrol, search and rescue and fishery protection, to name but a few. Trials with Airship Industries Skyships have been undertaken successfully by the French Navy, the US Navy and Coast Guard and the British Ministry of Defence, proving the ability of an airship to patrol for very long periods away from base, carrying search radar and other advanced avionics, and even carry/lower/retrieve an inflatable boat with boarding party to intercept suspect vessels.

Left: US Navy Hawkeye touches down on a carrier deck with arrester hook lowered.

The Royal Navy's OPV 3 requirement for an off-shore patrol vessel of the future is being contested by conventional surface craft and the Skyship 7000 or a derivative, the latter expected to carry weapon systems and Ferranti Seaspray radar for searching for and tracking of small surface targets in low visibility/high sea conditions. Control would be by fly-by-light fiber optics, as first tested on a Skyship 600 in 1986. A similar craft could also contest the US Navy's NASP (Naval AirShip Program) against contenders from Boeing and Goodyear, a program which could be worth $6 billion and cover 40 to 100 airships. With both OPV 3 and NASP, the airship would be expected to work with the fleet, resupplying and refueling from the ships. Airship Industries is teamed with the US company Westinghouse for NASP; the latter provides the APY-2 surveillance radar for the E-3 Sentry AWACS aircraft and will supply a derivative for the NASP airship.

There are many other forms of force multiplier and other external factors which will have profound effect on the design of fighters and bombers of AD 2000. Indeed, both attacker and defender will need the support of force multipliers if their missions are to succeed, taking many forms from data links and other electronic systems to manned refueling tankers and aircraft specifically intended to acquire targets and provide mid-course guidance for long-range missiles launched from bombers and ships.

This first chapter has given some insight into the problems confronting aircraft designers and crews in connection with future wars. It has attempted to explain the reasons why designers now put such emphasis on combat aircraft with 'low observable' (stealth) technology and why new methods have to be developed to elude the elaborate defenses of today and the future. The strange airframe shapes that appear later in this book have not been born from designers and artists allowing their imaginations to run wild, but adhere to strict technical parameters.

With AD 2000 less than a decade and a half away, it would be wrong to suggest that only warplanes of shapes peculiar to today will be seen in the skies. While this concept would produce a book of spectacular forms and images, it would not represent the true future picture. Many current warplanes will have been abandoned before AD 2000 but others in service will still be operational. Obvious examples of the latter are the US Navy's F-14 Tomcat, for which there is no planned replacement and which will continue in production in F-14D form well into the 1990s, the Soviet Tu-26 *Backfire* supersonic bomber, the AV-8B Harrier II and the European IDS Tornado. Indeed, the Harrier II will be typical of the least stealthy warplanes of AD 2000, its metal fuselage and large unshielded engine fan providing a marked contrast to the smooth-lined, all composite-constructed types to be built in series in the 1990s.

Much of the technology to produce 'low observable' warplanes is already known, though even the new US/USSR bombers make only partial use of it. But there are aircraft flying today that take the technology far beyond even those prototype fighters of Gripen and Lavi type that were still to fly at the time this was written. Of course they are shrouded in secrecy. At Lockheed's famous so-called 'Skunk Works,' the company has built prototypes of an amazing single-seater which is thought to carry the USAF designation F-19 and the acronym Cosirs (covert survivable in-weather reconnaissance strike). Several prototypes have been built under contract from the USAF's Flight

Left: Airship Industries Skyship 600 during trials with the French Navy. Future roles for airships could include AEW, antisubmarine and SAR.

Right: Tethered unmanned aerostats can also act as force multipliers, able to carry air, maritime and battlefield surveillance radars. This TCOM System 365 is in Nigerian markings.

Below: The F-19 could have configurational similarities to the Loral Corporation's conception of a stealth combat aircraft as shown here, with foreplanes and rear main wings, upper air intakes and exhaust venting, a blended fuselage and inward-canted tailfins.

Dynamics Laboratory, funded by the Defense Advanced Research Projects Agency of the Department of Defense. The first F-19 is believed to have flown as long ago as 1977. Probably powered by two 16,000lb (7257kg) thrust General Electric F404-GE-400 turbofans and capable of cruising at twice the speed of sound, it may have an SR-71A-type blended airframe evolved to offer minimum drag and high speed while keeping kinetic heating as low as possible. The engines are contained within the flat-looking rear fuselage, with root air intakes at the rear wings visible from above only, and conventional exhaust nozzles replaced by shielded vents in the fuselage upper surface. By keeping the orifices above the fuselage and adopting twin small canted-inward fins, the chances of strong radar reflection and infra-red and optical signatures are greatly reduced. Retractable foreplanes are likely and the aircraft is said to be transportable by C-5 Galaxy when its wings are folded. It is likely to be similar in size to the US Navy's Hornet but with a smaller wing span and lighter owing to advanced constructional methods. Whether or not the F-19 will become an operational aircraft is open to speculation and to date no photographs have been released.

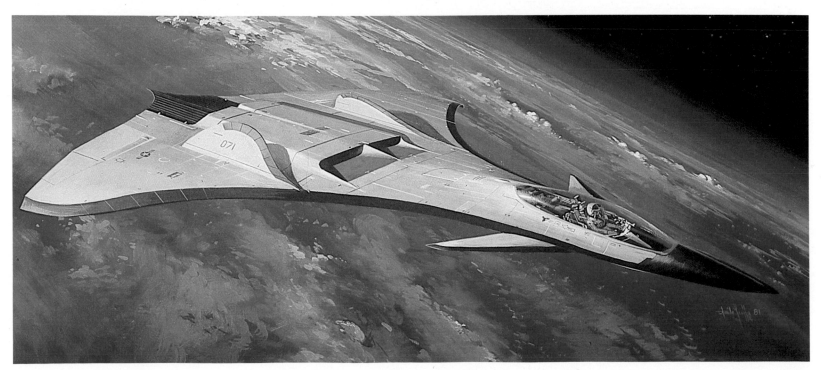

The suggestion that aircraft designers should try to make combat aircraft less 'visible' on hostile radars was made in Britain 50 years ago, yet until recently it was almost ignored. Designers call the apparent size of an aircraft, as seen on radar, the RCS (radar cross-section), which is the size of perfectly reflected flat metal plate, held square-on, which would look the same as the bomber on an air-defense radar screen. Obviously the very act of designing a jet bomber for high speed and the lowest possible fuel consumption makes it streamlined, so the RCS ought to be much less than the total frontal area. The RCS of the Boeing B-52H, for example, is around 107sq ft ($10m^2$), a high figure partly because the radar can 'see' straight in the engine inlets to the large first-stage fans of all eight engines.

To show the kind of improvement possible, the original B-1A prototypes cut the RCS to one-tenth ($1m^2$), and the B-1B now in USAF service cuts this again to only $0.1m^2$. Thus a formation of 100 B-1Bs would look roughly the same on an enemy radar as a single B-52H! By the 1990s the USAF will probably have a B-2 in service. At present known only as the Northrop ATB (Advanced Technology Bomber), this is the first bomber known to have been designed from the start for minimum RCS, or,

in modern language, using 'stealth' or 'low observable' technology. Details are classified, but it has been guessed that it might have an RCS only about one-thousandth that of the B-52, or a mere $0.01m^2$. In other words the entire bomber would look the same on radar as a metal plate of $0.01m^2$ size, or roughly the size of a pocket diary!

But the ATB is not the first aircraft known to have been designed according to 'low observable' principles. Back in the late 1950s the Lockheed 'Skunk Works' began planning an amazing spy plane to cruise at over 2000mph (3200km/h) and be hard to detect, which eventually materialized as the SR-71A Blackbird. Not only is it specially shaped, both externally and under the skin, to have the lowest possible RCS, but it is covered with special dark blue paint containing billions of microscopic iron balls which conduct electricity and help to nullify any reflection of radar waves. Much more recently the same design team, led by Ben Rich, created an even more 'invisible' aircraft, the Lockheed F-19 (as mentioned at the close of chapter 1). This is so secret that the USAF has never even acknowledged that it exists. It almost certainly has an RCS even smaller than that of the ATB, because though earlier in conception it is much smaller.

Previous pages: Fighter design optimized for high Mach supersonic cruise flight with a blended wing-fuselage, advanced turbofan engines carried in the wing roots and with vectoring/reversing nozzles, close-coupled foreplanes and variable camber wings, conformal weapons carriage, and advanced ECM.

Opposite: A sister aircraft to the Lockheed SR-71A Blackbird was the YF-12A fighter, possessing the performance and general configuration of the reconnaissance aircraft but which did not enter service.

Below: One of several Grumman impressions of a stealth fighter, with a very flat underside, sharp chines along the fuselage sides and no deep angles, engine intake above the fuselage and special nozzles, ideal for minimizing radar signature.

In 1986 it is easy to think of stealth as being a very special way-out technique used in just two very special aircraft. Nothing could be further from the truth. Long before the year 2000 it could be extremely hazardous for a military aircraft of pre-stealth design to fly close to any well-defended enemy position. This applies not just to fighters and bombers but to everything that bears air force or navy markings. Hostile sky is going to be deadly, especially for aircraft which are detectable.

The obvious way to remain undetected, apart from flying at night in the worst weather and at the lowest practical height, is to be a stealth design. This means making every part of the aircraft reflect radar waves anywhere but back towards the direction from which they came. The SR-71A, for example, has a very flat underside, sharp chines along the sides of the fuselage and no deep angles at the junction of the wings and the nacelles or fuselage – everything seems to flow into everything else. Clearly the shape also had to be right for speeds over 2000mph (Mach 3.2), so the whole design was quite an achievement – to say nothing of the need of most parts to work reliably at almost red heat! Inside the skin it is said that the structure is specially arranged to make deep V-shaped angles. Radar signals are bounced off the diagonal walls dozens of times, and as a large fraction of the energy is lost at each reflection practically nothing reaches the innermost point of the angle to be reflected out again.

Future combat aircraft, and eventually even maritime patrollers, transports and tankers, will have to be stealth designs. Wings will blend smoothly into the fuselage, no engines will be visible (though inlets may, provided radar energy gets 'lost' inside the duct) and the entire machine will be as devoid of protuberances or fins as possible. The obvious need to avoid going near a runway if a V/STOL type, or to be capable of very short take-off runs, means that full engine thrust must be available for takeoff and landing, which in turn means that wings can be almost non-existent. For cruising at high speed most of the lift can come from the body, and engine bleed jets (as used in hovering flight) can replace foreplanes, rudders and other projecting control surfaces.

But so far we have studied only the RCS. The paint scheme must not only be radar-absorbent but must also make the aircraft as invisible as possible at optical wavelengths. It is easy to make an aircraft almost invisible when viewed against a background of gray cloud, and similar colors (so-called air-superiority grays) are also hard to see against blue sky in some conditions of lighting. What makes selecting color camouflage difficult is that the same aircraft has to be hard to see when flying low over snow, or green fields, or the ocean. What about brilliant white contrails? Clearly there is no point in any of the efforts if the enemy is going to detect the IR heat energy from the engine(s).

Right: Grumman adopted a Northrop F-5A forward fuselage section and nose undercarriage, plus F-16 main undercarriage units and other 'off-the-shelf' components to reduce the cost and time involved in building its FSW demonstrator.

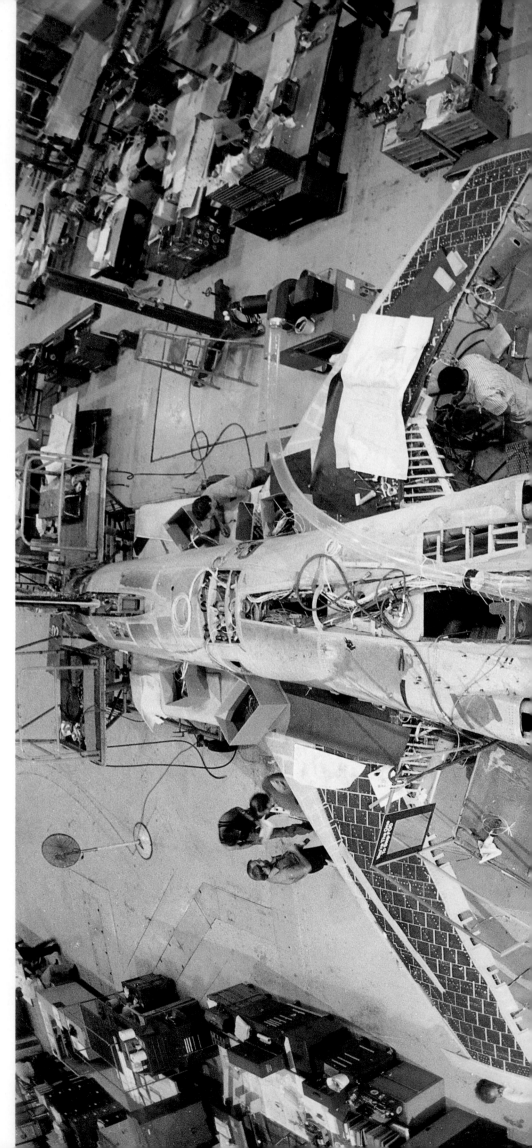

Some recent artwork from the USA has depicted supposed fighters of the 1990s and beyond. Almost without exception they are in full afterburner, blasting out an incandescent jet of supersonic flame. No more obvious way of inviting immediate destruction could possibly be imagined. It is very hard to throw away such images and instead imagine fighters with quiet, cool non-afterburning engines, but by AD 2000 new aircraft are going to have to try to be invisible to the eyes, quiet to the ears and so cool (literally) that there is nothing to excite the sensitive detectors in the waiting hostile missiles. We should not be misled by the some-times erratic performance of the infra-red homing missiles of yesteryear. Even the AIM-9L Side-winder missiles used by the Sea Harriers in the Falklands put up a nearly flawless performance against aircraft which invariably had no after-burners or were not using them (to conserve fuel). By the 1990s the next generation of AAMs will be designed to lock on unfailingly to fighter jet engines not in afterburner, so long before the year 2000 the engines of the newest warplanes will have to be both cool and shrouded by masking struc-tures. But fast jets cannot be fitted with compre-hensive suppressors such as those on today's attack helicopters (the Apache is an example), and trying to protect warplanes with powerful pulsed IR lamps is a very unstealthy activity.

A little thought shows that designers may also have to eliminate smoky jets and glint from a shiny canopy. In the mid 1930s many fighter pilots fought angrily against being cooped up inside an enclosed cockpit. By AD 2000 they might have to fight against being shut up with no outside view at all, except a synthetic one. Already US Army heli-copter researchers have suggested that before long helicopter crews will have to fly with what they call a 'virtual cockpit,' where transparent windows are replaced by a totally synthetic display created by sensors and computers. Such a display could show the real world outside (simplified), as well as enemy defenses (with their danger zones pictured) and the best track for the machine to reach the target. Superimposed on the display would be numerous numbers, symbols, pictures of its own missiles and other consumable items, and every-thing else needed to fly the mission. At first it would need much faith and nerve to fly a real mission under the treetops without seeing out, but this is thought to be the way helicopters must go.

The same may well become true for fighters and bombers. It has been suggested that the ATB will be an all-wing aircraft, because Northrop was pre-viously the world leader in such design. It would be particularly easy to put the crew inside the wing with totally synthetic cockpit displays. Even though a small canopy might look tiny compared with a big flying wing, it needs only a small glint of reflected sunlight to betray the bomber's presence.

It is paradoxical that the best stealth designs appear to be either almost no-wing or all-wing. The most aerodynamically efficient aircraft are such machines as the Airbus 310 or Boeing 767-300, which have small wings and giant bodies. On the other hand, when in 1949 the Northrop YB-49 fly-

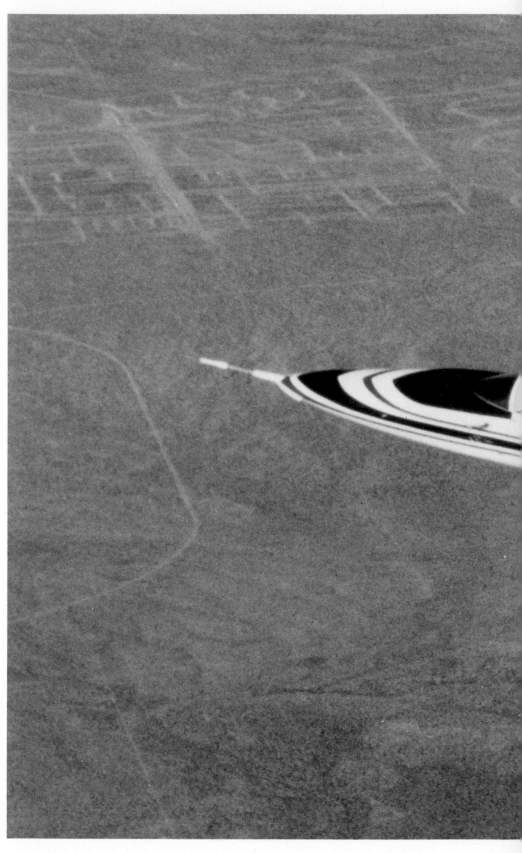

ing-wing jet bomber was competing against the big-bodied and more conventional B-36, it was the Northrop that – on the basis of available figures – showed most efficiency. At this point it is difficult to say whether the AD 2000 bombers and fighters will mainly be all-wing or look like needle-nosed lengths of piping. Certainly the flying wing could be expected to maneuver better than the length of pipe, but the whole idea of remaining undetected is that violent maneuvers are not called for.

In the past there have been many warplanes

Above: F-29A FSW demonstrator in flight.

whose pilots could open a roof hatch, raise their seat and get a better view for landing; this was even a feature of the lumbering Heinkel bombers of the Battle of Britain. Something of the sort will probably be arranged for Warplane 2000, the cockpit roof perhaps hingeing open like an inverted bomb bay to give the pilot direct external vision. On the other hand, long before AD 2000 the quality of the synthetic displays, covering the entire forward sector to at least 45° on each side, will probably be so marvellous that there will be no need for direct

vision. A major factor is that the synthetic external picture will be fed by sensors operating at many wavelengths from visible light, through IR to various radar wavebands, so it will be almost unaffected by night or any kind of bad weather.

After suggesting that Warplane 2000 might be wingless, it may seem odd to discuss the wing shape; but we did say it *might* be all-wing. The pioneer Northrop flying wings were slightly back-swept, but – to the amazed disbelief of many – the Grumman X-29A forward-swept wing demon-

strator that first flew in December 1984 is not only flying but delivering the goods, and suggesting that there is nothing about a straight-wing or swept-back aircraft that an FSW (forward-swept wing) cannot do better. The point must be made, however, that an FSW tends to need a canard foreplane mounted close in front of it, and canards threaten to spoil the stealth 'invisibility.' Perhaps if one always remembers that, unless it looks like a piece of stovepipe, Warplane 2000 must look as if it has been run over by a steamroller, even canards can be accepted. They would have to be lined up with sharp chines on a very flat 'squashed' fuselage which further aft blended into the forward-swept wing. Certainly the flat-body canard/FSW would have outstanding dogfight agility, especially with vectoring of the entire engine thrust, but it is very hard indeed to imagine how such a thing as a classical dogfight could take place in AD 2000 between the most up-to-date warplanes. One of the aircraft would inevitably be known to be in hostile airspace, which would mean swift destruction, though probably not by the enemy involved in the dogfight.

In 1936 a British driving instruction booklet was made more readable by cartoons of misguided drivers. One was pictured saying 'I'm terrified of crossroads, I go over them as fast as I can.' This is very relevant to Warplane 2000. Do we creep and crawl through enemy airspace stealthily? Surely we would do better to 'go into burner and dash for it?' On present evidence it looks as if stealth is the only answer, but it becomes more difficult when several aircraft have to fly together. Even though formations on the scale of World War 2, or even Vietnam, are gone for ever, there will be occasions when airlift demands, tankers and supporting air-craft will put a dozen aircraft in fairly close proximity, and doing this without being detected by any means whatsoever is no small challenge. It may well be impossible, even by AD 2000.

Such intruding formations would probably need station-keeping radar, terrain-following radar and some form of intercommunication, all of which could be detected. The alternative, of maintaining absolute silence, creates severe demands for high-precision navigation, detailed knowledge of the enemy terrain ahead, and even knowledge of every mast, guy-cable, power line and other obstruction, without daring to use an obstacle-warning sensor (other than purely passive IR, which is harmless).

Of one thing we may be sure: the next decade will see plenty of argument. In a recent listing of key technologies for the future of (military) aero-nautics Dr Robert S Cooper, Director of the US Defense Advance Research Projects Agency, started with 'No 1, stealth; No 2, supersonic cruise and maneuver.' Looked at from the imperfect tech-nology of 1986, these two key technologies appear to be incompatible; but time will tell.

Left: Artist's impression of an Advanced Tactical Fighter (ATF) in Forward Swept Wing (FSW) configuration, with rotatable air intakes to reduce the lower quadrant radar signature during high-speed flight.

Newton laid down a law that to every action there is an equal and opposite reaction, and this is true also in the realm of human conflict. With civil aircraft, developments in avionics are normal, the criterion being to make flight safer at an affordable cost. Military avionics, however, are grossly distorted by the fact that they are not intended to help the enemy. By AD 2000 the hostile sky will have become so perilous that the only way any flying vehicle – even an artillery shell – can survive will be by trying to remain undetected. The more avionics fitted, the harder this objective becomes.

Avionics (aviation electronics) is a vast subject, responsible for typically 35 to 45 per cent of the price of all the latest combat aircraft. Literally, these aircraft cannot fly without them. If a pilot yearning for the simple life tried to fly with everything switched off he would find his cockpit dead and lifeless, with the instrument displays as useless as a switched-off TV, his controls not connected to the aircraft and the throttle not connected to the engine. The mass media may perhaps be forgiven for thinking high-technology engineers and air marshals waste the taxpayers' money playing with expensive toys, but in fact nothing could be further from the truth. In an atmosphere of desperate shortage of defense funds, every new item has to justify its existence. Making a fighter

more expensive simply means that fewer of them can be afforded!

There may still be a few who hanker after the 'good old days' when levers in the cockpit were connected to the item at the other end by cables, push/pull rods and rotating-torque tubes. The notion that everything has to be connected via fiber-optic digital data buses may seem ridiculous, but there is no future alternative. If we went back to the old ways we would have to give up almost every mission capability possessed by even today's fighters, let alone tomorrow's, and we would come out with an airplane that was bigger, heavier, more expensive and dramatically less reliable.

Avionics in combat aircraft can be divided into many categories. The most obvious are the sensors used for navigation, for finding the enemy and for guiding weapons against him, by day and night and in every kind of weather. Other avionics are used to communicate with 'friendly' forces on land, sea, under the sea, in the air and in space. Offshoots from communication include Elint (electronic intelligence) systems, to listen in to everything the enemy is doing, and IFF (identification friend or foe), which keeps friend from destroying friend. Within the aircraft are a host of systems which control the aircraft's flight, manage all its complex systems (including the afore-

Previous pages: An EL/L-8202 advanced self-protection jamming pod pylon mounted on a Kfir fighter, incorporating beam-sharpening techniques and a threat library.

Below: Elta EL/M-2001B airborne ranging radar fitted to a Kfir tactical fighter, able to operate in conditions of heavy ground clutter.

mentioned sensors and communications) and link every part of the aircraft with the cockpit on the one hand and with various recording systems on the other. The recording systems keep track of every part of the aircraft and measure the number of flights, the number of operating hours, keep a detailed history of every time anything has been overstressed (for example, an engine turbine which may have been briefly overheated) and the percentage of the total life of each part that has been used up, while giving instant warning as soon as any potentially dangerous condition arises which could cause an important part to fail.

Though the 'equal and opposite reaction' inevitably means that many sensors help not only ourselves but also the enemy, the fact remains that warplanes cannot fly useful missions without them. In theory, a pilot could fly over an enemy target well into the next century and drop a bomb in a dive attack without using any sensors other than his unaided eyes. In practice he would be shot down long before he got near the target. Already the way to penetrate hostile airspace is to fly at the lowest practical level, to try to avoid detection by hostile radar and to try to avoid emitting any detectable signals, while perhaps choosing for the purpose the worst combination of night and bad weather.

Until the 1980s many air forces, not even excepting the USAF, adhered to the view that they could economize on sensors and get by with just basic navaids (navigation aids) and a simple weapon-aiming sight. Long before AD 2000 every user of combat aircraft must have accepted that, even in so called 'limited wars,' it is essential to operate round the clock and in the worst weather, and to fit the very best weapon-aiming systems.

Invariably the biggest sensor is a radar, and – while the highly specialized radars used in AEW and surveillance aircraft will always be enormous – radars fitted to combat aircraft have tended to get slightly smaller in size while growing dramatically in capability. By the 1990s every radar will have at least a dozen operating modes, each selectable instantly to suit the particular task or mission function. A radar, of course, consists of two main visible parts, the boxes and the antenna. The boxes consist of the power supply, signal generator, transmitter, receiver and other items including the cockpit display, plus some form of cooling system. The antenna usually takes the form of a circular or elliptical dish or flat plate which is mechanically scanned (pointed in different directions) like a searchlight. The boxes and aerial are connected by waveguides, rectangular-section metal tubes along which the special microwave signals travel.

One of the shortcomings of most fighter radars is that when they are angled down to see the ground the giant reflection from the ground makes it impossible to see anything very close above it. For example, fighters of 1950s-origin flown today cannot 'see' a hostile aircraft streaking along at a height of about 200ft (90m) unless the fighter is itself at this very low height and can detect the enemy against or above the skyline. Fighter radars now in production have special 'pulse doppler' techni-

ques which can instantly spot anything moving across the background, so when backed up by new missiles they have what is called 'lookdown, shootdown' capability. This is fast becoming universal for all fighters, though there are problems. Back in the early 1980s F-15 fighters of the 36th TFW at Bitburg found their radars were locking on to BMW and Mercedes cars speeding along nearby autobahns. Resetting the MTI (moving-target indication) circuits to cut out everything moving at less, than, say, 130mph (210km/h) means that in wartime the F-15s might fail to spot hostile helicopters. By the 1990s radars will be more advanced, and will be able to tell a helicopter from a fast car.

Certainly all attack and bomber aircraft will have DBS (doppler beam sharpened) radars, with special signal processing to give 'pin sharp' pictures resembling a good monochrome photograph. Even more amazing definiton can be obtained with the SAR (synthetic-aperture radar) in which a computer sends out the signals in such a way that they appear to have come from a radar with a gigantic aerial hundreds of feet across. Giant radars naturally can display a better and more detailed picture than small ones, but they cannot be fitted into a fighter. With the SAR, future attack aircraft will get the best of both worlds. By AD 2000 many aircraft will use radars of the next generation still, in which DBS synthetic-aperture pictures are created by a conformal-array radar. In this the aerial is built in to form major parts of the airframe. Conformal arrays, which would use computer-controlled electronic scanning instead of mechanical scanning, promise to revolutionize the 'fine-grain vision' of small aircraft.

Of course, the 'action and reaction' problem means that if we pump out radar signals they make small jets behave like flying lighthouses, betraying their presence. There is no point in having a radar if it has to be switched off to avoid being detected.

Above: In support of the US Navy's Cover Optical Landing System, GEC Avionics has supplied thermal imaging equipment for evaluation on board a US Navy aircraft carrier. This enables the deck crew to 'see' an incoming aircraft's approach even in total darkness. The thermal image of an F-14 Tomcat fighter on a monitor is seen here. The image appears in 'black and white' as shown.

Left: Linescan 4000 images can be recorded on film for later analysis.

Right: GEC Avionics FLIR pod, which provides the pilot with night vision.

Ask some attack and helicopter pilots what they do today to try to overcome this problem and they will often answer 'Turn the wick down,' in other words reduce radiated power. This naturally results in a degraded picture and reduced range, and is especially unhelpful if the radar has to penetrate heavy rain or snow, smoke or fog, or enemy jamming (part of the technique of ECM, electronic countermeasures). Today the radar laboratories are developing highly classified LPI (low probability of intercept) techniques which will enable fighters of the 1990s and the twenty-first century to use high-power radars without much chance of alerting the enemy. Most LPI techniques have already gone into use with communications radios, where whole messages can be stored in a computer and then transmitted in a thousandth of a second in a stream of pulses which hop from one frequency to another almost at the speed of light.

Tomorrow's fighters and bombers will certainly be able to 'see' over a far broader range of the EM (electromagnetic) spectrum than any of their predecessors. The shortest EM radiation commonly used is visible light, which is utilized by the crew's eyes and by stabilized optical magnification systems. Next comes the vitally important broad spread of frequencies known as IR (infra-red), which is the same as heat. At still longer wavelengths come the radars, beginning with the millimetric midgets and passing up through the centimetric wavelengths to the long metric waveband, which has not been much used since the end of World War II.

There are some fundamental differences between these sensors, all of which are certain to be used in future combat aircraft. Those which work at optical frequencies use light (originating from the sun, moon or stars) reflected or scattered from the target. Even on the darkest night there is always some light available, and by the 1990s image intensifiers and LLTV (low-light TV) will be able to

Below: The British Aerospace Linescan 4000 is an infrared surveillance system for operation by day/night in bad visibility. Images can be shown in 'real time' on the pilot's display or transmitted to a ground station.

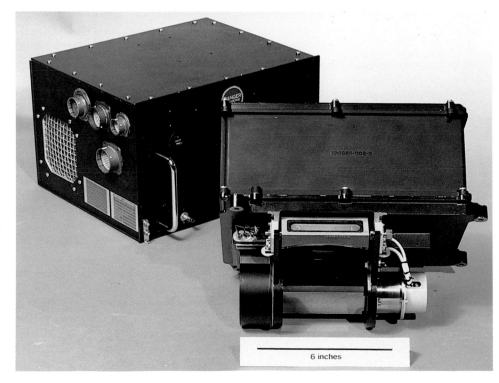

6 inches

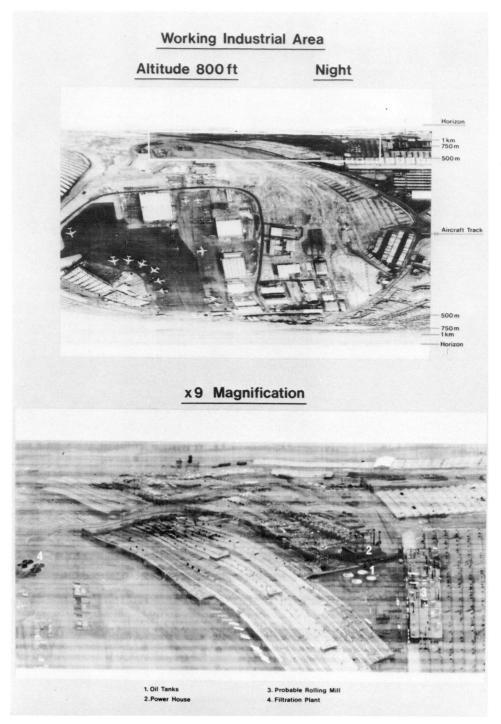

Working Industrial Area

Altitude 800 ft   **Night**

Horizon
1 km
750 m
500 m

Aircraft Track

500 m
750 m
1 km
Horizon

x9 Magnification

1. Oil Tanks
2. Power House
3. Probable Rolling Mill
4. Filtration Plant

Above: Linescan image of an industrial area taken at night from an altitude of 800ft. The boxed section in the upper photograph was selected for further investigation, with magnification of ×9 still producing a clear image.

give the pilot a bright picture even in seemingly dark conditions. IR devices work in a totally different way. They measure the temperature of everything in the target scene, presenting the result in shades of gray from white to black. Usually cold parts of the scene are black and hot ones white, but the display can be switched the other way round. Obviously this kind of sensor could function in total darkness, and it works because everything on Earth is actually at quite a high temperature (relative to absolute zero); thus a winter scene at 0 degrees C can more accurately be written as being at 273K, degrees Kelvin being measured relative to absolute zero. A hot desert might be at 310K and a tank's exhaust pipe at around 600K. Thus the IR, often called FLIR (forward-looking IR), has plenty of temperature differences which show up in a detailed monochrome picture.

Radar works by sending out pulses or waves and

studying the reflections. Thus though it has always been more common on warplanes than image intensifiers, FLIRs and LLTVs, radar is the only one that is active (self-emitting). The others are passive (non-emitting), and it is a fair bet that by AD 2000 almost all sensors will either be passive or be LPI radars of such cunning design that the enemy cannot detect them.

Communications, navaids, ECM and EDP (electronic data processing) are all going through major upheavals, but by AD 2000 they should have settled down in new forms. It seems prehistoric to realize that squadrons now on the flightline use such navaids as ADF and Tacan. Even the INS (inertial navigation system), which came in seemingly a short while ago with the F-104G, has been totally rethought and by AD 2000 will be used almost exclusively in the LINS form (L for laser), using novel 'gyros' in which two sets of laser light race each other in opposite directions round small plastic triangles with mirrors at each 120° corner. All INS species have the great advantage for a combat aircraft of being totally self-contained.

Doppler radar, which measures drift and groundspeed by reflecting thin beams off the Earth's surface ahead of and behind the aircraft, clearly is one of the undesirable 'aerial lighthouses' that warn the enemy. Despite this it has been very popular, and even for 1990s fighters new forms of cunning LPI doppler are being developed which it is hoped will make good the very small slow drift of the INS, which makes the INS progressively less accurate the longer the mission lasts. In any case the USA has developed what can fairly be called the perfect navaid, GPS Navstar. Fully operational from 1988, it will use a constellation of 18 satellites orbiting slowly at high altitude in groups of six on three different orbits. On board will be super-accurate atomic clocks, and carefully encrypted signals highly resistant to being jammed or utilized by an enemy. (In any case the Soviets will have a very similar system, Glonass.) The signals will be detected by every 'friendly' user – aircraft, spacecraft, ships, tanks, even infantry – and everyone will always know his precise speed and position. Navstar could be used by a Tiger Moth to drop a bag of flour inside a 5-foot circle without looking at the ground, and it could then steer the same light biplane back to a perfect blind landing in a small field. Clearly it is going to have no small effect, but there is one snag. It belongs to the USA. Suppose British forces had got used to it at the time of the Falklands war? The USA, wishing to stay neutral, might have changed the codes to prevent British use. No nation can really afford to base its war planning on a foreign system.

Of course, if our 2000-era aircraft were foolish enough to pump out any kind of detectable emission – such as radar signals or jet heat – the enemy could shoot them down without using any active emitters of their own. So far, however, national air defense systems have needed radars, radio communications and even radar-guided missiles. All of these are to some degree susceptible to enemy ECM, and after decades of neglect today's combat aircraft are becoming equipped to handle various

kinds of ECM. The simplest form is jamming by chaff, the name given to bundles of fine aluminized glass threads which, when released, 'bloom' in a second or two to form giant clouds which reflect radar much more strongly than the carrier aircraft. Chaff can be sized to match the known wavelengths of particular hostile radars, but today most fighters carry prepackaged cartridges which, as soon as the pilot receives a warning that his aircraft is being 'illuminated,' can be fired rather like a shotgun. Tomorrow's fighters will be cleverer. Their RWR (radar warning receiver) will include a threat library of all known hostile emitters. When the RWR detects signals from an enemy radar it will compare the signals with those stored in the library. It will take no action unless it confirms that the signal comes from a hostile antiaircraft system of a deadly kind which could shoot the aircraft down within seconds. Only then would it issue a warning, store the emitter's exact location (for a future attack) and then proceed to pump out a chaff cloud cut to the exact length on the spot to have maximum effect.

Other countermeasures include miniature radio sets forming short-term active jammers as powerful as major radio stations, and flares which burn brightly to present a juicy target for IR-homing missiles which might otherwise prefer the aircraft's jetpipe(s). All can be packaged in standard cartridges fired from an ECM 'eggbox.' There is still argument about how such ECM should be installed. In the past most have been built into streamlined pods hung on pylons or 'scabbed' conformally on the skin of aircraft, but many experts believe that in the 1990s and beyond all ECM will be internal. Certainly it seems to be foolish to use one or even two of a small number of stores pylons to carry defensive ECM, but the contrary view (widely adhered to in the RAF) is that it is undesirable to load a small fighter with internal devices that may only occasionally be needed. Common sense would seem to suggest that as ECM would be needed on nearly 100 percent of missions in any future war, there is every reason for making them a neat internal fit, leaving the pylons for the weapons and auxiliary fuel tanks.

Above: Fighting helicopters also use forward looking infrared systems. The US Army's Apache carries a Target Acquisition and Designation System (TADS) in a rotating nose turret for the gunner to use for search and detection by way of direct view optics, TV or FLIR, and laser designation. A Pilot's Night Vision Sensor (PNVS) using a forward looking infrared system carried in an above nose turret allows nap-of-the-earth flying in poor visibility by providing guidance symbology in a monocle ahead of one of the pilot's eyes.

In spite of predictions concerning the stealth, or 'low-observable,' design of fighters and bombers for AD 2000, the truth is that not a great many of the world's warplanes are really likely to be of such futuristic conception by then, though many will benefit from various aspects of the technology. Although the technology will be available, as much already is, current programs and defense budget restrictions for R&D and purchase will ensure that probably only the USA and USSR will deploy full stealth warplanes by that date in any worthwhile number for strategic and the most critical tactical roles. These uses will include reconnaissance, which is vital and would be as difficult to perform over well-defended enemy territory as, say, bombing.

France, Britain and others may well have partial or full low-observable fighters and fighter-bombers flying as prototypes in the 1990s, but operational deployments may take longer than for the superpowers who appear to require a higher level of preparedness. Interested European nations could collaborate on the development of such a warplane, to spread the enormous cost and ensure a high level of production, but this would be best with the full co-operation of France and recent difficulties in agreeing the design of the less sophisticated EFA (European Fighter Aircraft) may be taken as an omen.

Another possible direction could be that the USA will become the major supplier of very high-technology warplanes to the West and other countries, as the USSR is the major supplier to the Warsaw Pact and others. This would not indicate a decline of European manufacturing, as companies in Europe would contribute skills and components to these warplanes while continuing with their independent programs related to aircraft on which they had indigenous interest or an unquestioned lead. For Britain the latter could relate to the development of a supersonic Harrier.

Previous pages: Dassault-Breguet and Dornier have developed an advanced attack version of its Alpha Jet trainer known as the Lancier, with FLIR, multifunction nose radar, internal passive and active ECM and other upgrades to give it extended day and night capabilities against other aircraft (including helicopters), and land and sea targets. Not yet in service, the Lancier certainly will be still around in AD 2000.

Opposite: HiMAT is launched from a B-52 bomber at an altitude of about 45,000ft (13,715m).

Below: HiMAT (Highly Maneuverable Aircraft Technology) is a Remotely Piloted Research Vehicle (RPRV), about half the size of a 1990s fighter and intended to flight test various advanced features before they are incorporated into future combat aircraft. Built by Rockwell International for NASA and the USAF and capable of above Mach 1.5, its aim is to enhance the transonic maneuverability of future US fighters and is said to demonstrate maneuvering performance 60 percent better than current fighters.

This overall picture is not intended to give the false impression that there will be a void period between now and the coming of the super high-technology low-observable warplanes. It can be argued that the full low-observable types are for most nations two generations away, current warplanes now in service being complemented, or superseded, by an interim generation. Interim in this case should not be taken to mean 'stop gap,' for these warplanes represent a quantum improvement over existing types and some are yet to fly even as prototypes.

Before taking a closer look at the individual aircraft that can be grouped under the heading 'European fighters,' it is interesting to note some of the research projects currently being undertaken in Europe and elsewhere which will have a profound effect on future fighters. Although in an earlier chapter it was said that stealth design and violent maneuverability may be considered mutually incompatible in the twenty-first century, in the shorter term the quest to proceed along the path of outmaneuvering the enemy in the conventional way remains strong.

No better example of this can be found than with the US Advanced Fighter Technology Integration (AFTI) programs, which cover many different aspects of future technologies. One aircraft testbed used in the AFTI programs is a General Dynamics F-16. The F-16 itself is, of course, very advanced in 1980 terms, using a fly-by-wire flight control system in place of 'old hat' mechanical linkages. The quad-redundant system has allowed the aircraft's center of gravity to be moved to the rear in accordance with the CCV (control configured vehicle) principle of relaxed static stability, greatly reducing the fighter's drag at supersonic speed and at high load factors. The fly-by-wire system manages this by linking the pilot's controls electronically with the aircraft's moving control surfaces, a computer integrating the inputs from the controls and sensors monitoring the dynamic forces on the airframe to ensure that the normally opposing considerations of handling qualities for the pilot and the best aerodynamic shape for the airframe are compatible by artificial means. An even more advanced system is fly-by-light, which uses fiber optics to link pilot controls and movable surfaces, offering an even greater weight saving plus higher survivability in war and immunity to electromagnetic pulse.

The revolution in microprocessing allowed the 1970s generation of fighters to become extremely sophisticated, giving the crew plenty to do and, conversely, making serviceability more difficult. The new trend is for easing the pilot workload, ironically through the development of even more advanced but simpler cockpit instrumentation systems. How this is translated to the next generation of fighters is described later in this chapter. However, with the AFTI F-16 not only are many of the cockpit systems extremely advanced but two large foreplanes are carried under the fuselage on the engine inlet duct to offer unique flying modes in association with special avionics. In addition to the usual maneuvers, the pilot of the AFTI F-16 can

Below: An F-16 used in the Advanced Fighter Technology Integration (AFTI) programs.

Above: Night vision aid carried under the nose of a Westland Sea King, the pilot wearing a helmet-mounted display.

perform others beyond the capability of normal fighters. For example, it can perform what is called six 'decoupled' motions, aimed at putting the aircraft on the required flight path and in a 'firing' position in the quickest time. For example, if an operational pilot of today wishes to turn to starboard, he has first to roll into a bank, pull on the column to swing round the aircraft's nose and then roll out of the bank. The AFTI F-16 pilot can turn without banking by sliding sideways, the deletion of a roll enabling him to fire sooner, facilitated by the wings remaining level at all times.

This 'decoupled' motion is one of six. 'Decoupled' lateral motions are direct side force, yaw axis pointing and lateral translation. They are executed by the pilot using his rudder pedals, which activate the flaperons, foreplanes and rudder. Longitudinal 'decoupled' motions are axis pointing, vertical translation and direct lift, executed manually via a twist grip throttle (port) which activates the trailing-edge flaps and the tailplane. The pilot can choose 'decoupled' or conventional flight modes at will.

To further enhance the fighter's capabilities, the AFTI F-16 can demonstrate the ability to fly four entirely different types of combat mission without degradation of the aircraft's flight characteristics or combat efficiency. Using the control panel of his cockpit head-up display (HUD), the pilot can select the mission which immediately puts into effect the required control laws and sets up the radar, headup display, fire control computer, weapons man-

agement system and multipurpose displays commensurate with the role. Three digital computers comprise the hardware for the flight control system and new programs can be added. With the planned automated maneuvering attack system installed, the pilot could select to take control of the attack or leave it to the AMAS and flight control digital computers, or somewhere between the two extremes.

Another AFTI F-16 program will cover a technology that also encompasses control. This is known as 'Interactive Avionics,' which will be used in future warplanes. In what might appear extraordinary now, but is already demonstrable, cockpit warning lights will be superseded by an audible voice warning of emergencies, which the pilot will hear in his headset. Two obvious benefits are that the pilot does not have to take his eyes off the action ahead to register the warning and, secondly, that there is no chance of missing the warning. Taking this technology further, a prerecorded personalized cassette of voice commands could be loaded into the data transfer module for memory by the voice command computer. Checking first that the cassette matches the pilot's actual voice, the computer would then accept commands by voice, the pilot talking the aircraft's 'vocabulary' via his microphone. Confirmation that the order has been carried out would be shown on the two push-button multipurpose display units.

The data gained from these and other AFTI F-16 programs are being made available to the US aero-

Above: The commander of a tracked Rapier anti-aircraft unit wearing a Ferranti Helmet Pointing System (HPS). This directs weapons and sensors to targets viewed by the wearer.

Opposite: Co-bonded carbonfiber composite wing for the EAP (Experimental Aircraft Program).

Below: The EAP co-bonded wing, comprising the lower skin in panel with spars, is checked before being attached to the upper skin. This wing is being produced by Aeritalia.

space industry, forcing the pace of combat aircraft design and ensuring such systems will be operational by AD 2000. Helmet-mounted sights are already in use with military forces ranging from helicopter and tactical aircraft crews to the commanders of land-based anti-aircraft missile systems (such as tracked Rapier). For the AFTI F-16 the pilot is intended to wear a helmet sight that will enable him to acquire the target by centering crosshairs on it. The pilot can be looking in any direction, and once the crosshair lights illuminate (to indicate centering) he can instruct the radar or FLIR sensor to align automatically for 'lock on.' The missiles do the rest!

Recent major advances in structural materials have given designers a greater choice of structural properties and configurational possibilities, which will be reflected in the new warplanes of 1990s

service and beyond. Not only are there ultra-high-strength steels, titanium alloys and aluminum/lithium alloys, but a vast field of fiber-reinforced composites opens the way to 'tailoring' structures to have anisotropic (directionally oriented) properties. Like a sheet of thin wood veneer, sheets of composite can be made highly flexible in one direction and remarkably rigid in another. This is of more than academic interest. Already it has made possible the FSW (forward-swept wing) aircraft, flying in the form of the Grumman X-29A. Such wings appear odd because, as they could not be made in traditional materials – except in something like solid steel, with prohibitive weight – we are unused to seeing them. By the year 2000 they are likely not merely to be more common but possibly the preferred shape for combat aircraft. This is because the FSW combines good aerodynamics and aeroelastic features which make the resulting aircraft smaller, more agile and more efficient than any counterpart with swept-back wings.

An FSW has to have most of the plies (thin fiber-reinforced sheets) arranged so that the fibers are angled about 9 degrees forward of the angle of the leading edge. This forces the wing to bend upwards under air loads in such a way that its incidence does not increase. Thus it avoids catastrophic upward bending, called 'divergence' by engineers, which with a wing of traditional construction would cause immediate total failure. Future combat aircraft will use carbonfiber, Kevlar and possibly boron to make airframes lighter yet much stronger than ever before. In all cases the fiber directions will be calculated by computers to lie along the best directions to resist the flight loads.

In all these advanced composite materials the strength lies in the fibers; the bonding resin is merely the adhesive that sticks them together. The fibers have amazing strength because they are structurally perfect, whereas today's metal parts are highly imperfect because they consist of billions of small grains or groups of crystals. Each group of crystals has fantastic strength, but the joints are weak, like a wall that has poor mortar. For many years metallurgists have tried to make structurally perfect pieces of metal. Already perfect crystals of silicon and germanium are being produced (they are sliced into tiny pieces to make

Opposite: Active Control Technology (ACT) Jaguar demonstrator flies with the third production Tornado ADV. Note the position of the Tornado's tail control surfaces, showing maximum negative lift (a stable aircraft) and slight positive lift on the totally unstable ACT Jaguar.

Below: NASA AD-1 oblique-wing test aircraft.

Above: ACT Jaguar fly-by-wire installation, comprising four high-speed mutually self-monitoring flight control computers (four center boxes on ground), two actuator drive and monitor computers (on outside of ground row), pilot's control panel, three quadruplex gyro packs, a lateral accelerometer and five control surface transmitters.

Opposite: British Aerospace EAP technology demonstrator being towed from its final assembly point onto a weighbridge in No 3 Hangar at BAe's Warton Division in Lancashire, 27 October 1985.

'chips' for microelectronics), and now the latest aero engines have single-crystal turbine blades. The crystal joints are arranged along the length of these blades to resist the tremendous tensile load when the engine is running. Single-crystal blades can thus retain their strength to higher temperatures than traditional metal blades. What metallurgists have long wanted to do is make perfect flawless pieces of metal of a large size. Then we could lift a Jumbo Jet with a cable as thin as a human hair, we could build a bridge from England to France and we could build much, much better aircraft.

As mentioned, the forward-swept wing configuration has several advantages over back-swept wings, others including nearly spin-proof characteristics, lower stalling speeds, improved low-speed handling and lower drag across the operational envelope. The latter is especially important when nearing supersonic speed, allowing less powerful engines to be fitted, which in turn could be important for many reasons but including a lower infra-red signature.

Composite materials have allowed the USAF to fund a mission-adaptive wing program (MAW), in which an F-111 fighter-bomber has had its wings modified to use wing camber control instead of the aircraft's usual spoilers, flaps and slats. Glassfiber is used to produce a smooth, flexible and uninterrupted surface, internal mechanisms changing the contours of the leading and trailing edges during flight. In addition to a leading-edge movement range of up 5 degrees to down 30 degrees and a trailing-edge movement of up 7 degrees 30 minutes to down 25 degrees, the wings can be twisted spanwise. This control method produces improvements in performance due to the generation of very efficient airflows both under and over the wings. MAW is part of the AFTI series of programs and as such may indicate that a most modern

fighter of AD 2000 could be variable wing camber controled for certain flight conditions.

Another NASA program concerns applications of the oblique-wing concept to a future fighter for the US Navy, though this wing could equally well be used on other aircraft types including bombers. Following on from the NASA AD-1 experimental oblique-wing test aircraft that flew in 1979, it is intended to fit an oblique-wing to an F-8 Crusader fighter (used by NASA and already fitted with a digital fly-by-wire control system) in order to expand the research up to speeds probably in excess of Mach 1.4. In principle, the oblique-wing is seen as a replacement for the more complicated variable-geometry wing configuration, whereby a straight wing is pivoted so that it can be swung round during flight to angles of up to, say, 60-65 degrees fore and aft, producing the effect of conventional variable geometry without the complications of the usual heavier system. Future

applications will depend partly on demonstrable maneuverability. Quite clearly the oblique-wing would have advantages over conventional variable geometry beyond weight saving. These would include the availability of an entirely straight wing for take-off and landing, plus loiter, oblique angle wing for high-speed interception, and easier stowage on board ship with the wing in oblique position almost parallel to the fuselage.

Research into advanced fighter design is not, of course, confined to the USA and USSR, though we have few details on Soviet R&D. Other nations whose aircraft industries develop and build first-line combat aircraft have research programs of their own, including Israel and a host of European countries. British Aerospace, for example, flew the SEPECAT Jaguar Active Control Technology demonstrator in a program which saw the first flight trials in the world of a full authority quadruplex digital flight control system without

Above: Artist's impression of the completed EAP demonstrator.

any other form of back-up. Development of this fly-by-wire control system was an essential element in the program to build the EAP (Experimental Aircraft Program) fighter, which has its aerodynamics optimized for low supersonic drag and exceptional maneuverability at subsonic, transonic and supersonic speeds, achieved by the adoption of compound sweep wings and anhedral foreplanes, and high negative stability.

Stealth technology, researched by British Aerospace for several years, is incorporated to some degree into the EAP, and the aircraft's structure benefits from research carried out by the company and Aeritalia into carbonfiber composites (CFC) and new metal alloys. For example, the EAP wing is a co-bonded carbonfiber composites structure with the spars bonded directly to the bottom skin and the top skin bolted to the spar flanges. This reduces the need for mechanical fasteners and greatly increases wing strength. Super plastic

forming and diffusion bonding of titanium is also adopted for high strength components of EAP, and new lithium/aluminum alloys with superior structural properties are used in the airframe.

The EAP cockpit is optimized for single pilot operation in the projected future combat environment, with integration of all systems and displays. The system is computer controlled with information transmitted to the cockpit head-down color multifunction display CRTs via data bus highways, replacing conventional wiring. The three multifunction displays also show systems status, warnings, checklists and emergency procedures. An advanced holographic head-up display is used.

Associated with British Aerospace on the EAP are several other UK, Italian and West German companies, and some aspects of the design may find their way into the projected EFA (European Fighter Aircraft). Roll-out of the EAP took place in 1986 and it was anticipated that the demonstrator

Below: EAP pilot Peter Orme at the controls to check the cockpit environment.

would show acceleration and maneuver performance superior to all current combat aircraft. Maximum speed will be more than Mach 2.

A similar configuration to the EAP has been proposed by British Aerospace for the European Fighter Aircraft, though the EAP's technology will benefit any other fighter taken into service by the Royal Air Force in the 1990s should the EFA not get international approval. The EFA had been planned originally as a five-nation effort, France, West Germany, Italy and Spain joining Britain in its development and production. Planned service date was the mid 1990s. However, in 1985 France pulled out of the program.

EFA is planned by the remaining nations to be primarily an air-defense fighter, equipped with a multimode pulse-Doppler radar capable of acquiring eight targets simultaneously and directing advanced lookdown/shootdown and snap-up weapons such as AMRAAM and ASRAAM air-to-air missiles. STOL (short take-off and landing)

capability is considered essential and power will be provided by two advanced turbofan engines in the 20,000lb (9070kg) thrust class with afterburning. Maximum speed could be in excess of Mach 1.8. Attack would be a secondary role for the aircraft.

EFA will make extensive use of composite materials should it go into full development. A first flight could be achieved by 1990 or just after, and operational service could begin in or around 1995. Britain and West Germany each require some 250 examples, and Italy and Spain want 100 each, all totals including a number of two-seat variants for training purposes.

Working co-operation between Britain, Italy and West Germany has already been established on the Tornado program and it is entirely reasonable to expect an EFA to follow from the four-nation program. Interestingly, the EAP uses two Turbo-Union RB199 turbofan engines of the type fitted to Tornado. The Tornado will still be in operational

Above: The EAP cockpit was developed from a research program into cockpit integration, within which a range of functional cockpits with active displays was developed to allow layout and display presentation to be evaluated by aircrew and engineers during simulated missions.

Right: General arrangement of the EAP demonstrator.

British Aerospace's initial
design submission for the
European Fighter Aircraft
(EFA) project.

Above: Tornado GR.Mk 1 of No IX Squadron, based at RAF Honington carrying four 1000lb bombs and two drop tanks. It is among the most formidable strike aircraft in the world and will continue in service into the 21st century.

Left: The new and highly successful RAF Tornado F.Mk 2 air defense interceptor armed with four Sky Flash and two Sidewinder missiles and carrying drop tanks. The ADV will be one of the older interceptors in AD 2000.

Opposite above: The many roles expected of the Hawk series 200 aircraft include battlefield interdiction and antishipping strike, and export sales will probably ensure its continued service in AD 2000.

Right: The AMX will certainly be around throughout the 1990s, despite its conventional configuration and mostly aluminum alloy construction (carbonfiber fin).

service itself in AD 2000, though by then the international interdiction/strike version will be a fairly old design and the air-defense variant will be of less importance than any follow-up type in RAF service. What might keep the ADV Tornado in service longer than might otherwise be expected is its long-range autonomous capability to operate against multiple targets at night, in poor weather conditions and in an ECM environment, at over 400 miles from its airfield. To keep the ADV in good shape for the future, update programs will be required. One will see the replacement of Sky Flash and Sidewinder missiles with AMRAAM and ASRAAM and the associated multiplex digital data bus. The electronic combat and reconnaissance variant of Tornado will also remain in use in AD 2000 with the German Luftwaffe.

The current SEPECAT Jaguar will not be in RAF or French use by AD 2000, though international sales that continued in the 1980s, and Indian production, could mean that some Jaguars remain flying by the end of the century. France anticipates the development of an ACT (tactical combat aircraft) to supersede the Jaguar in the 1990s, the technologies for which are to be demonstrated by the Dassault-Breguet Rafale experimental combat aircraft. The Rafale will also demonstrate technologies for the similar ACM (*avion de combat marine*), the proposed combat aircraft to be deployed on board the French nuclear-powered

aircraft carrier *Charles de Gaulle* which was laid down in 1986. A second carrier could follow, as both the current vessels (*Clemenceau* and *Foch*) will require replacing in the 1990s. *Charles de Gaulle* could be commissioned in 1995. While the current carrier-borne Dassault-Breguet Super Etendard in French Navy service is being modified to carry the ASMP nuclear missile and there is reason to believe the French Navy might have the weapon systems of existing aircraft updated and extended, the tactical combat aircraft can be seen as a replacement type.

Rafale, which first flew in 1986, is generally similar in layout to the British EAP, though its composite constructed compound delta wings are of smaller total area and the foreplanes are further back on the fuselage and without anhedral. There are, of course, other differences in configuration, including the adoption of plain air intakes with splitter plates on the lower center fuselage, whereas EAP has rectangular intake ducts under the fuselage. Larger than the current Mirage 2000, Rafale has been designed to cope with several demanding roles, ranging from air superiority against all enemy aircraft (from supersonic fighters to armed helicopters) while carrying four Matra Mica medium-range air-to-air missiles and two Matra Magic close-range missiles (and an internally mounted gun) to ground attack with 'fire-and-

forget' stand-off or electro-optically guided missiles up to a typical weapon weight of 7715lb (3500kg) against targets 350 nautical miles from its airfield. In the air superiority role it has an all-up weight of just 30,864lb (14,000kg), made possible by the use of composites in its construction and ensuring a thrust-to-weight ratio much better than one. The composites include carbon, Kevlar and boron fibers. Aluminum-lithium alloys and titanium are also employed in the airframe, and manufacturing techniques include the super plastic forming and diffusion bonding method as used on the EAP.

Rafale's cockpit reflects the very latest forms of data display, including multifunction color displays and a wide-angle holographic head-up display. Fly-by-wire control is adopted but there is provision for the later use of fly-by-light to enhance survivability in a nuclear environment, and voice warning and control systems are also planned for the future. Power is provided by two 17,195lb (7800kg) thrust afterburning General Electric F404 turbofans and maximum speed will be around Mach 2.

A future Rafale type would complement French Air Force Dassault-Breguet Mirage 2000s still in service in AD 2000 and could well capture the lion's share of the international export fighter market in the way managed by the earlier Mirage

Above: The new-generation Dassault-Breguet Mirage 3 NG, with flight refueling probe fitted.

Above right: Dassault-Breguet Rafale experimental combat aircraft.

Right: A special display Mirage 2000 'Cristal,' showing what is found under the skin of the fighter.

A joint Italian and Brazilian program has been responsible for the Aeritalia/Aermacchi/EMBRAER AMX close support aircraft, which will begin to join the Italian Air Force and Brazilian Air Force in 1988 and 1989 respectively. Powered by a single 11,030lb (5000kg) thrust Rolls-Royce Spey Mk 807 non-afterburning turbofan, AMX can attain 723mph (1164km/h) and carry a warload of 8375lb (3800kg).

III. It is thought that neither the Mirage III nor the swept-wing Mirage F1 will be prominent in AD 2000 with any major air force, though the new generation Mirage 3 NG with its reconfigured delta wings, swept foreplanes, higher-rated SNECMA Atar 9K-50 turbojet engine, new avionics and fly-by-wire control system, could have established an international market position in the late 1980s that would allow its continued presence at least into the 1990s.

The Mirage 2000, first flown in 1978, is of fairly conventional delta configuration but will remain prominent through the 1990s by virtue of having become the French Air Force's primary combat aircraft from the later 1980s. It has also been exported in considerable numbers. It is powered by a single 21,385lb (9700kg) thrust with after-burning SNECMA M53-P2 turbofan, and maximum speed is above Mach 2.2. It can achieve a rate of climb of 56,000ft (17,060m) per minute and has an ultimate g limit of +13.5. All this means that a Mirage 2000 can intercept an enemy aircraft flying at Mach 3 and at the very high altitude of, say, 80,000ft (24,385m) in under five minutes from the time of releasing its brakes at its base.

The single-seat Mirage 2000C1 interceptor and Mirage 2000B two-seat trainer version are joined by the two-seat Mirage 2000N, a two-seat attack version conceived to undertake low-altitude penetration raids while carrying, perhaps, the ASMP air-to-surface nuclear missile. Strengthened

to allow a typical mission speed of 690mph (1110km/h) while flying at only some 200ft (60m) above the ground using its terrain-following radar, the 'N' will enter French service from 1987 and replace Mirage III-Es and nuclear-armed Jaguars. Eventually the French Air Force alone may have well over 300 Mirage 2000s of the various models in service, of which substantial numbers will be operated in AD 2000.

Both the Mirage 2000 and the Mirage 3 NG have fly-by-wire control systems but use far fewer composite components than the Rafale generation of combat aircraft. The design and fabrication of composite components is far from easy and some aircraft manufacturing nations wishing to incorporate such technology into their next generation combat planes have had to seek the advice and assistance of foreign companies with greater experience. British Aerospace at Warton, for example, began research into carbonfiber composite structures as long ago as 1966. It was to capitalize on this experience that Saab-Scania of Sweden decided to team with BAe in the joint design, test and assembly of the carbonfiber wings for its JAS 39 Gripen combat aircraft.

It was Saab's development of the tandem-winged fighter concept that introduced the rear main wings and foreplanes configuration to our modern skies, its Viggen becoming an extremely capable multirole aircraft with above Mach 2 performance and the ability to reach a height of

Right: Two-seat trainer Mirage 2000 B has a second cockpit but retains operational capability.

Below right: At industry expense, Dassault-Breguet developed a scaled-up Mirage 2000 as the Super Mirage 4000, powered by two M53 turbofan engines and suited to interception and penetration strikes at far greater ranges than the Mirage 2000, largely thanks to approximately three times the internal fuel capacity. Marginally faster than the Mirage 2000 and with a better rate of climb, it has nonetheless not been ordered to date.

Below: Dassault-Breguet Mirage 2000 C1 carrying two Magic air-to-air missiles and two AS 30 Laser tactical air-to-surface supersonic missiles to attack hardened targets.

Right: Saab JA 37 Viggen tandem wing fighter in latest blue-gray camouflage, flown by a pilot from F13 Wing of the Swedish Air Force, based at Norrköping.

Left: Models of the Saab JAS 39 Gripen in F13 Wing markings.

Below: Cockpit layout for the JAS Gripen, with a Hughes wide field of view diffraction optics Head-Up Display (HUD) to present critical flight symbology while simultaneously permitting a clear forward view. Ericsson Radio Systems AB is responsible for the cockpit displays, with three head-down displays and back-up instrumentation.

10,000 meters from standstill in under 1 minute 40 seconds. Unfortunately for the company the Viggen did not attract export orders, even though it came very close when put into competition with aircraft like the US F-16 for European service.

In 1985 the Viggen remained in production in JA 37 single-seat interceptor form, five of 17 planned Viggen squadrons of the Swedish Air Force still requiring the type. However, by AD 2000 the Viggen replacement program will probably be eight years into effect, with as many as 115 single-seat and perhaps 25 two-seat training Gripens in service.

Gripen was conceived for the same basic uses as previous Saab combat aircraft, namely *jakt*, *attack* and *spaning* or, translated, fighter, attack and reconnaissance. It is lightweight, in the tradition of the Saabs, with a normal take-off weight of only about 17,635lb (8000kg). This is achieved by nearly one-third of its airframe comprising composite components. Like the Viggen, it will be able to use roads as runways in times of emergency and is designed to be very simple to maintain to ensure high levels of serviceability. Turnaround servicing could even be undertaken mainly by conscripts.

The first two prototypes, to be flown in 1987, have carbonfiber wings constructed by British Aerospace. These are of cropped delta planform, ahead of which are mounted close-coupled swept

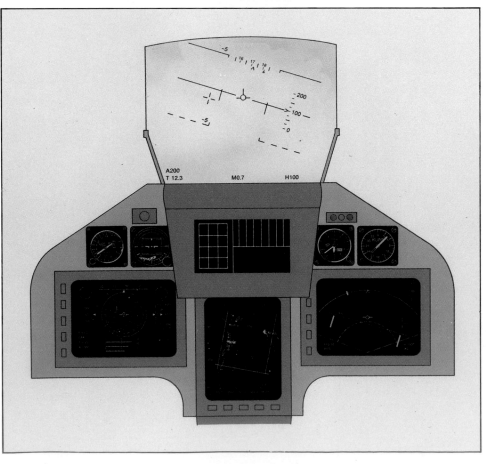

foreplanes. A triple-redundant digital fly-by-wire control system is used, and cockpit displays include a Hughes Aircraft diffraction optics head-up display and three SRA head-down displays. The three head-down displays have quite distinct purposes: the port display replaces the conventional instrumentation of older aircraft types, though the Gripen prototypes carry some conventional instrumentation for back-up use if required; the central display gives a computer-generated map of the area being over-flown and has superimposed tactical information; while the starboard multisensor display relates information from the radar and forward-looking infra-red (FLIR) equipment. The Gripen's pulse-Doppler radar is much smaller than that in the Viggen but has a 300 percent increase in functions. Apart from the 27-mm Mauser automatic cannon carried in the fuselage, the Gripen can carry six air-to-air missiles, electro-optically guided missiles and other ground attack weapons, or reconnaissance pods for use by day or night.

Power for each of the Gripen prototypes is provided by a single 18,000lb (8165kg) thrust with afterburning General Electric/Volvo Flygmotor RM12 turbofan. Performance data have not been released but it is known that Gripen is supersonic at all altitudes. Given a much lighter weight and smaller size than the Viggen but also a far less powerful engine (Viggen in JA 37 interceptor form has a 28,100lb [12,750kg] thrust with afterburning Volvo Flygmotor RM8B turbofan), the prototype Gripens may have a similar performance to the EFA (European Fighter Aircraft).

Gripen is therefore another future combat aircraft that will be in its heyday in AD 2000 but will not be of the full stealth design as tested by F-19, though possessing many very advanced technologies. Perhaps more speculative is the future production of the Swiss Piranha 6, as under development by a team of scientists under the collective company name Arbeitsgruppe Für Luft-und Raumfahrt or Aerospace Task Group. Typically an aircraft with rear-positioned compound delta-type wings and foreplanes, no doubt including much composites in its airframe structure and with the latest in avionics up to the required operational standard, it has been conceived to offer those air forces not able to afford the most expensive combat aircraft a high-technology supersonic single-seater for multimission use. Principal roles could include clear weather air defense at low and medium altitudes using beyond-visual-range air-to-air missiles, and forward-edge of battle area low-level strike with more than 7715lb (3500kg) of attack weapons and flying usually under visual flight rules (VFR) conditions, reconnaissance and electronic warfare. On the power of a single RB199 Mk 104 afterburning turbofan engine of Tornado ADV type, it could attain Mach 1.8 and possess a maximum rate of climb with half fuel weight and cannon ammunition of over 59,000ft (18,000m) per minute. One of several radar choices is the Ferranti Blue Vixen multimode coherent pulse-Doppler with look-up and lookdown/shootdown and beyond-visual-range all-weather capability. Maxi-

Right: Cockpit mock-up for the Piranha 6.

Top left: Model of the Swiss ALR Piranha 6, a future supersonic combat aircraft particularly suited to nations not able to afford the more expensive new-generation warplanes.

Center left: Piranha 6 model undergoing subsonic wind tunnel tests.

Bottom left: Wind tunnel testing shows flow over a Piranha foreplane surface.

mum take-off weight is estimated to be 22,045lb (10,000kg). No date for the first flight of a prototype has been reported at the time of writing.

The Blue Vixen radar will form an essential part of the Royal Navy's BAe Sea Harrier mid-life update program, which covers modifications to 30 aircraft by 1990. Other changes include the ability to carry four AIM-120 AMRAAM 'fire-and-forget' advanced medium-range air-to-air missiles, cockpit display updates and changes to the controls, an

improved radar warning system and secure voice and data links. The first updated Sea Harrier FRS Mk 2 flew in 1986. The ability of the updated Sea Harrier to lookdown/shootdown is of major importance, as this lack of capability (due to the Blue Fox multimode radar in the initial production Sea Harrier FRS Mk 1s) was demonstrated to be a handicap during the 1982 Falklands conflict.

With updates to the Sea Harrier lasting until 1990, plus export sales, it is likely that the Sea Harrier will still be in service at least close to the end of this century. By then a supersonic counterpart might have been developed. However, this may well depend as much on the US Navy/Marine Corps seeing the need for such an aircraft (perhaps to supersede the F/A-18 Hornet) as on a Royal Navy requirement, even though BAe, McDonnell Douglas, Rolls-Royce and Pratt & Whitney are all undertaking R&D. Development of a supersonic V/STOL type would pose no insuperable problems technically but the cost would be very high indeed. Therefore a supersonic V/STOL aircraft equal in performance at least to the Hornet will probably have to wait until, say, AD 2010.

There are several engine concepts under consideration for a supersonic V/STOL, all with their own possible benefits. Many believe the best to be the 'plenum chamber burning' single-vectored-thrust engine, which is not unlike the existing Pegasus but has combustion in the front nozzles. This arrangement promises high thrust-to-weight ratio and plenty of power at supersonic speeds.

Right: Ferranti Blue Vixen multimode coherent pulse-Doppler radar.

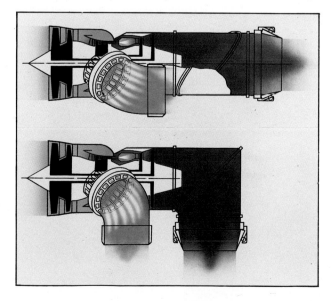

Above: A Sea Harrier makes a STO (Short Take Off) using the 'ski-jump' method.

Left: Artist's impression of mid-life update Sea Harrier FRS.Mk 2s with Blue Vixen radar and AMRAAM missiles, enabling the aircraft to meet threats into the 21st century.

Because V/STOL (vertical/short take-off and landing) aircraft offer several advantages over conventional fixed-wing aircraft the Harrier family and derivatives are likely to play important roles even in AD 2000. The most obvious are that the Harrier family can operate even after runways have been destroyed, and offer combat capability to navies without in-service (or the funding to commission) large aircraft carriers for fixed-wing warplanes. Naval V/STOL aircraft can be recovered without the carrier having to turn into wind and, because catapults/arrester gears are not required for launch/landing, recovery takes less time. As V/STOL types can operate from very small platforms, they can offer over-the-horizon reconnaissance and strike capability to naval vessels not originally intended to carry fixed-wing aircraft, and can fly from ships and take up station on land without needing an airfield or even a long clearing.

Right: Illustration of the Plenum Chamber Burning (PCB) thrust augmentation system. The Pegasus 11 engine with PCB would give a thrust rating of 27,000lb (12,247kg), a substantial increase over the current engine and suited to a supersonic V/STOL combat aircraft.

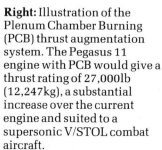

Sea Harrier FRS.Mk 1s flown by the Royal Navy, one carrying AIM-9L Sidewinder missiles.

Left: The McDonnell Douglas Model 279-3 is just one conception of a possible supersonic replacement for the Harrier, its PCB Pegasus engine having four vectoring nozzles.

Center left: Many believe the only survivable combat aircraft in a future major war would be those able to be dispersed away from airfields and not requiring runways, as both would be targeted by an enemy at the outbreak of hostilities. This means V/STOL, but as an aircraft can carry more weapons/fuel with a short take-off run than in a vertical lift, the true answer is STOVL (Short Take Off and Vertical Landing). The British Aerospace P.1214-3 seemed to give the best of all worlds, having STOVL capability combined with supersonic performance and high maneuverability through thrust vectoring and forward-swept wings, but this has not been officially backed to date.

Bottom left: Another of many artist's conceptions of a possible future supersonic vectored-thrust fighter, this time with an F-16 influence to the airframe configuration but with an engine layout suited to the role and outrigger wheels retracting into mid-wing fairings.

Right: US Marine Corps AV-8B in vertical flight.

The US Marine Corps, Soviet Navy, Royal Air Force, Royal Navy and the navies of Spain and India already appreciate the benefits of V/STOL fixed-wing combat aircraft and it appears others may follow suit. For example, the new Italian aircraft carrier *Giuseppe Garibaldi* (commissioned in 1985) has provision for V/STOL fixed-wing aircraft and carries a 'ski jump,' though none has been ordered. Both the US Marine Corps and the Royal Air Force, plus the Spanish Navy, are currently taking into service examples of the latest version of the Harrier – known as the AV-8B Harrier II, Harrier GR.Mk 5 and EAV-8B Harrier II respectively by the operating countries. Replacing

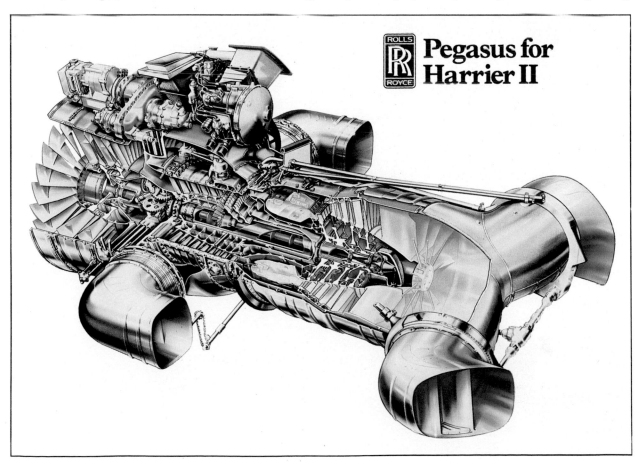

Right: Cutaway of the Rolls-Royce Pegasus 105 vectored-thrust turbofan engine being fitted to the RAF's Harrier GR.Mk 5.

Above: AV-8B Harrier IIs flown by USMC Squadron VMA-331.

Left: One way to remove the need for runways is to operate aircraft from water. In the 1950s Convair built a small series of experimental delta-winged and turbojet-powered seaplane fighters for the US Navy Bureau of Aeronautics. Known as Sea Darts, these were the first seaplanes to exceed the speed of sound.

Above right: The two-seat demonstrator Harrier used in Skyhook/crane retrieval tests.

Right: The Lockheed Hydro-Star can be viewed as a modern version of the Sea Dart, combining current stealth technology with the retractable hydro-ski take-off method so successfully demonstrated by the 1950s fighter.

the original Harrier in the longer term, the Harrier II is a joint US/UK effort under the companies McDonnell Douglas and British Aerospace.

Harrier II, like the original Harrier, is a close-support aircraft and so does not have the nose-mounted radar of the Sea Harrier fighter. The AV-8B version uses a 21,550lb (9775kg) thrust Rolls-Royce F402-RR-406 vectored-thrust turbofan engine, the RAF Harrier GR.Mk 5 a 21,750lb (9865kg) thrust Pegasus Mk 105, both with the new well documented rotatable nozzles for vertical and horizontal flight. A night attack version of the Harrier II will be flown in prototype form in 1987. Compared to the Harrier, the Harrier II has larger area supercritical wings of graphite epoxy composite construction with leading-edge root extensions (LERX), larger trailing-edge flaps and drooped ailerons. Sections of the fuselage, most of the tailplane and the rudder are of similar composite construction. The AV-8B's instantaneous turn rate is higher than for the original Harrier and its weapon load is greater at a normal maximum of 9200lb (4173kg).

In AD 2000 the Harrier II and probably the Sea Harrier will be operational, though in updated forms, the latter having its military usefulness increased not only by modification but by the development of new handling techniques. For instance, British Aerospace and Dowty Boulton Paul have been conducting experiments with the so-called 'Skyhook' system, whereby Sea Harriers can be launched and recovered by even small ships in conditions of up to sea state 6. Using the specially designed pick-up device on the end of a crane, the ship is able to 'capture' the aircraft in flight and then swing it on board to be placed on a rearming trestle or stowed away. The pilot's task is to formate on a stabilized hover sight which guides him to the contact window, sensors judging when the actual lock-on should take place. Lock-on, rearming and launching via the crane could be performed automatically if desired. It is envisaged that Skyhook could be used to refuel aircraft at sea or give many sizes and types of naval vessel aircraft-operating capability. The trestle system, power supplies and so on could be installed on existing and future vessels not designed to carry aircraft, which would be an especially useful asset in wartime for convoy escorting, or could be designed into new ships with below deck hangar space for standby aircraft.

The following chapter begins with the Soviet equivalent to the Harrier, but it is very revealing to note that as far as is known the Soviet Union is not developing a replacement for its Yak-38 *Forger* and some US planners are said to consider aircraft with STOL capability preferable to V/STOL fighters, as the latter have weight penalties not considered by these planners as cost effective. However, other experts suggest that, with runways a prime target for enemy attack at the very outset of war, only a V/STOL or STOVL (short take-off and vertical landing) aircraft can guarantee to remain operational to continue the fight, the short take-off capability being useful to enable a greater warload to be lifted than during vertical operations.

The Soviet Yakovlov Yak-38 *Forger* V/STOL probably will not be operational in AD 2000, and production has been extremely limited by Soviet standards (thought to be about 60 aircraft to date). Though *Forger* has proven capable of short take-offs as well as vertical (which were not considered within its capabilities by Western observers some years ago owing to the power plant arrangement of one large Lyulka turbojet engine with two vectoring nozzles and two separate Koliesov engines exhausting downwards to perform as lift-jets), it is considered less useful than its counterpart in the West, the Harrier.

Forgers currently operate from the four Soviet *Kiev* class tactical aircraft carriers, which provided the Navy with its first true carrier battle group capability. Development of *Forger* has continued and modifications to the airframe have been observed, but it is thought unlikely that any are used as tactical aircraft on land, as are RAF Harriers, and they will probably not be seen on board the new *Kremlin* class nuclear-powered aircraft carriers operational from the early 1990s. Of course, a completely new V/STOL combat aircraft cannot be ruled out for the 1990s onwards but the main candidates for *Kremlin* vessels appear to be Sukhoi designs, the Su-24 *Fencer* Mach 2.18 variable-geometry attack two-seater and the new single-seat Su-27 *Flanker* all-weather counter-air fighter, both in special navalized forms.

The first of perhaps eight nuclear-powered aircraft carriers is nearing completion at the Niko-layev 444 shipyard on the Black Sea. It has a displacement of approximately 75,000 tons, is 1100ft (335m) in length, and is covered with weapon systems and sensors. For initial trials a navalized version of the Mikoyan MiG-23 *Flogger* might be used, but this aircraft will be out of date by the time full operational deployment is achieved and will have given way to *Flanker* or a similar new generation fighter. Indeed, *Flogger* and its predecessor, the MiG-21 *Fishbed*, will be of little or no importance by AD 2000. Mock carrier deck trials have taken place at an airfield close to the Black Sea using a concrete 'deck,' the aircraft observed using it having included the Sukhoi Su-25 *Frogfoot* subsonic attack aircraft. However, neither *Frogfoot* nor its US equivalent, the Fairchild Republic A-10 Thunderbolt, will be in much evidence as the end of the century approaches.

Attempting to assess what Soviet fighters will be around in AD 2000 is made all the more difficult by the secrecy surrounding the development of all 'super stealth' type aircraft currently being worked on by the superpowers. It can safely be assumed that the Soviets have their own F-19 types under development. These will be seen in the West only as they are viewed by satellite while under test just before operational deployment or are subsequently abandoned and perhaps exhibited at Monino alongside such advanced aircraft (for their time) from the past as the Sukhoi Mach 2+ cruise bomber, *Bounder*, the Tu-144 supersonic airliner and the record-breaking MiGs.

Previous pages: F-15C Eagle air superiority fighters. Eagles will remain in USAF service for some time after the ATF has entered squadrons.

Below: Soviet Navy Yakovlev Yak-38 *Forger-A* V/STOL combat aircraft on board ship with outer wing panels folded upward.

Above: Kiev Class aircraft carrier *Novorossiysk*, its on-board weaponry including four twin SS-N-12 (NATO *Sandbox*) long-range antiship missiles (as seen on deck, with reload facility).

Right: Artist's impression of the nuclear-powered aircraft carrier *Kremlin* being built at the Nikolayev 444 shipyard on the Black Sea. This vessel and its sister carriers to be built will have great influence on naval warfare in AD 2000.

By AD 2000 the MiG-21 will be history, while the MiG-23 will have given way by 1990 or thereabouts to the MiG-29 *Fulcrum* and Su-27 *Flanker*. The Mach 3.2-capable Mikoyan MiG-25 *Foxbat* will also probably be a casualty of time, being levered out by the superior MiG-31 *Foxhound*. These three newer aircraft represent a new generation of Soviet fighters, all of which will gain increasing prominence as we head towards the next decade and beyond.

Fulcrum can be judged as the Soviet equivalent of the US F-16 Fighting Falcon, though its design appears to have incorporated a large pulse Doppler radar with lookdown/shootdown capability from the start. This radar bestows day-and-night all-weather operation, even against low-flying enemy aircraft and cruise missiles. Similar lookdown/shootdown capability for *Foxhound* and *Flanker* means that Soviet pilots no longer have to rely on ground control to effect difficult interceptions.

Though of advanced design and clearly intended to match Western fighter technology, *Fulcrum* is still of mainly metal construction, with compound sweepback to the wing leading edges and with twin outward canted tailfins/rudders. It is powered by two 18,298lb (8300kg) thrust with afterburning Tumansky R-33D turbofan engines, which allow an estimated maximum speed of Mach 2.2 at high altitude and above Mach 1 at sea level, while possessing a thrust-to-weight ratio of above 1 and a sustained turn rate superior to all previous Soviet

fighters. Missile choices include six AA-10s, the latest radar homing weapon that fills the previous gap in the medium range.

Fulcrum first entered Soviet service in 1984 and have also been delivered to India. The fighter will clearly be entering service with Soviet-friendly nations over the forthcoming years.

At Gorkiy, production is under way of the MiG-31 *Foxhound*, which can be regarded as a direct development of the MiG-25. As has been well documented, the MiG-25 was developed originally to counter the threat posed by the US North American B-70 Mach 3 cruiser bomber being proposed as a B-52 replacement. Although the B-70 program was abandoned in 1961, development of the Soviet fighter continued. Interceptor and reconnaissance models of the MiG-25 were produced. While the aircraft's Mach 3.2 'clean' and Mach 2.83 armed maximum speeds made it virtually interception proof and an ideal aircraft for Voyska PVO air-defense units, its radar became outdated when faced with the new threat of low-flying cruise missiles.

Soviet *Foxbat-As* were later fitted, therefore, with radars capable of limited lookdown/shootdown technology already incorporated into the MiG-23 *Flogger-B*, the first Soviet fighter able to track and engage targets travelling at heights below its own. The modified *Foxbats* became 'E' variants, and engines were uprated to an incredible 30,865lb (14,000-kg) thrust with afterburning. However,

Right: Mikoyan MiG-25M *Foxbat-E* interceptor flown by the Voyska PVO.

Center and bottom right: Two of the first released photographs thought to show a pre-production version of the Sukhoi Su-27 *Flanker* fighter.

Below: US Department of Defense impression of a Mikoyan MiG-29 *Fulcrum* fighter with AA-10 missiles escorting a *Backfire* bomber.

Foxbat-E can be viewed as the provisional answer and *Foxhound* the ultimate solution.

Foxhound began entering Voyska PVO units in 1983. Though generally similar in configuration and structure, with the same Tumansky R-31 turbojets, it is heavier, a two-seater instead of a single-seater, has a lengthened fuselage and different air intakes. Most important of all, *Foxhound* has an advanced lookdown/shootdown radar with track-while-scan, a radar comparable with that fitted to the US F-14 Tomcat. This radar is allied to new AA-9 long-range radar homing missiles with a reported range of up to 28 miles (45km). In trials *Foxhound* has intercepted targets flying at under 200ft (60m) altitude and above 70,000ft (21,300m), in the latter case the target flying at some 15,000ft (4575m) above the altitude of the fighter. *Foxhound* is thought to have a maximum speed of Mach 2.4 and a ceiling of 80,000ft (24,385m).

The Sukhoi Su-27 *Flanker* is the Soviet equivalent of the US McDonnell Douglas F-15 Eagle and has a radar with lookdown/shootdown and track-while-scan comparable in performance to the F-15's AN/APG-63. It was first observed by satellite at the Ramenskoye flight test airfield and was then given the provisional Western name Ram K. When it was clearly seen to be a production type, NATO gave it the name *Flanker*. Operational deployment with the Soviet forces began in 1985.

Flanker's radar has been tested against simulated targets during many trials at Vladimirovka, a testing airfield close to the Caspian Sea. Like *Fulcrum*, it is a single-seater and intended for counter-air duty, though possessing attack capability. Production is centered at Komsomolsk. Construction is thought to be conventional and in configuration *Flanker* has swept-back wings, uncanted twin fins/rudders and large air ducts below the wingroots. Its two turbojet engines are reportedly derived from the Tumansky R-31. Much heavier and larger than the MiG-29, *Flanker* is believed capable of Mach 2.34. Its radar is said to be capable of a range of 150 miles (240km), with tracking at up to 115 miles (185km). Six AA-10s are *Flanker's* main air-to-air weapons.

Both the MiG-29 and the Su-27 reportedly carry infra-red search and tracking equipment, cockpit head-up displays (HUDs) and digital datalinks, bringing them to the level of the best Western fighters. Su-27s are expected to supersede Su-15 *Flagon* delta-wing interceptors operated by the Voyska PVO, and become important tactical aircraft on land and in navalized form at sea. As for the current Mach 1.65 Tupolev Tu-28P *Fiddler*, first seen in public in 1961 and recognized as the largest interceptor ever put into operational service anywhere, and the equally old Yakovlev Yak-28P *Firebar* all-weather interceptor with afterburning Tumansky R-11 turbojets carried in nacelles under the swept wings, both will diminish from their current operational levels (estimated at 120 and 150 respectively) within the Voyska PVO and will be out of service well before AD 2000.

Fiddler's range (with maximum fuel load) of some 3100 miles (4990km) has offered the Soviet home defense forces a long-range interceptor

Left: Sukhoi Su-24 *Fencer-C* variable-geometry attack aircraft, introduced to Soviet units from 1981.

capable of dealing with an enemy well away from Soviet borders. It is doubtful, therefore, whether *Fiddler* will be retired until a replacement has been found, and some Western experts speculated that Aircraft 101 could be such a type. Aircraft 101 was known to be a horizontal tailless delta, powered by four 44,092lb (20,000kg) thrust turbojets. In July 1983 it established no fewer than 14 world records, including averaging a speed of Mach 1.91 around a 1000-km closed circuit while carrying a payload. It subsequently became clear that Aircraft 101 was not a huge interceptor but either a variant of the Tu-144 supersonic airliner or the Sukhoi (or an unknown Antonov) cruise bomber. However, the size of the aircraft should not in itself be taken as an indication that it was improper to consider Aircraft 101 as an interceptor. Unless the Soviet Union decides to develop a new *Fiddler* replacement, it is very likely that a bomber will be modified for the task. Candidates could include the Sukhoi Su-24 *Fencer*, though some experts in the West talk about the huge Tupolev *Bear* in this role. Despite the age of its design, *Bear* is still being built as a missile carrier, and its impressive weapons capability and ability to carry a huge radar would justify it also as a *Fiddler* replacement. As many experts now agree, speed is not the essential factor for an interceptor any more, so long as its radar and missiles have sufficiently long range to attack enemy aircraft at a reasonably long distance.

Left: The US Navy's Tomcat carrier-borne multirole fighter will still be in service in F-14D form in AD 2000.

Before the turn of the century replacements for the Soviet Sukhoi Su-17, -20 and -22 series will also have been found for ground attack and fighter roles, though what form these will take is as yet unknown. The Su-24 *Fencer* Mach 2.18 variable-geometry attack aircraft, which first entered Soviet service in 1974, is a slightly smaller and lighter US F-111 lookalike and will certainly be active through the 1990s. It can therefore be speculated that development has already begun, or will begin shortly, of composite-material stealth-technology fighters as long-term replacements for *Fulcrum* and *Flanker* (though both will be much in evidence in AD 2000) and of new attack aircraft with greater weapon load capability than the current Sukhois, and that a *Fiddler* replacement might take the form of a converted bomber. What is certain is that the Soviet Union will continue its uninterrupted program of fighter development, even while funding such immensely expensive projects as space-defense systems and despite the likely cutbacks in US advanced military aircraft programs caused by the SDI program. *Flanker*, *Fulcrum* and *Foxhound*

may have already matched Soviet fighters technically with those of the West, and the pursuance of well-funded R&D could see the West lagging behind in fighter technology by AD 2000 or at least in the production of operational aircraft in sufficient numbers.

A clearer indication of what types of fighter are likely to follow those currently on the production lines can be gleaned from looking closely at US programs, realizing that the USA and USSR have similar aims. It is generally recognized that the Soviet Union produces a new fighter every six years or so, though the type to be superseded may remain in service for many years thereafter. An example of this is *Fulcrum*, which is entering service gradually to supersede not only the previous MiG-23 *Flogger* but also the older MiG-21 *Fishbed*. While recent successive Soviet fighters have incorporated radical changes in configuration, it is reasonable to say that each has been a mix of established and new technologies, bringing about a completely new generation fighter only every two or three designs.

Below: F-14 Tomcat of Navy Squadron VF-51 launching an AIM-54 Phoenix, the longest-range air-to-air missile in operational use. From the 1990s Tomcat will carry AIM-120 AMRAAM and AIM-132 ASRAAM to supersede Sparrow and Sidewinder.

In the West since the frivolous 1950s, new fighters have been adopted only every 12 years or more. This has had two major effects. Firstly, a new Western fighter has tended to be a new generation type rather than just an improvement, and secondly it has had to be capable of dealing not only with the current threat but that posed by maybe one or two later Eastern bloc models.

Unlike the Soviets, the US has fighters at sea and on land. The US Navy currently relies upon the Grumman F-14 Tomcat, a Mach 2.34 variable-geometry carrier-based two-seater. It is powered by two 20,900lb (9480kg) thrust Pratt & Whitney TF30-P-414A turbofan engines and carries the Hughes AN/AWG-9 weapons control radar capable of detecting airborne targets at ranges up to 195 miles (315km). The AWG-9 can also track 24 targets simultaneously and handle attacks on six targets even when they are at different ranges and heights and in an ECM environment. The primary weapon for Tomcat is AIM-54 Phoenix, the longest range air-to-air missile that is capable of over Mach 4 and more than 124 miles (200km). The new AIM-120A AMRAAM 'fire-and-forget' medium range missile will supersede Sparrow shortly on Tomcat and other US fighters, which also carry Sidewinder for short-range attacks.

Tomcat in the initial F-14A form entered US Navy service from 1972 and some 26 squadrons were operational by 1986, mostly deployed on board 12 aircraft carriers. By AD 2000 the US Navy will have three further carriers in service, namely *Theodore Roosevelt*, *Abraham Lincoln* and *George Washington*. The demise of the Navy's oldest carriers will not reduce its planned 15-carrier force by the early 1990s, as the Navy has carriers currently used non-operationally for training or in reserve.

As Tomcat is expected to remain in production into the 1990s and will serve in the twenty-first century, update programs have been initiated to produce the improved forms F-14A (Plus) and F-14D. No plans to develop beyond the F-14D have yet been formulated. The former is basically the F-14A with new General Electric F110-GE-400 engines having scaled-up fans and incorporating exhaust nozzle components from the F404 engine as used by the Hornet. This engine change allows the Tomcat a very significant increase in thrust, while reducing fuel consumption with afterburner and thereby improving range/endurance. Take-offs can be effected without the use of afterburning.

With the F-14D, which will be the main version of Tomcat by AD 2000, the power plant update will be joined by the installation of the new AN/APG-71 radar and digital avionics. The latter will include new weapons management, navigation, cockpit displays and control functions. The radar will have monopulse angle tracking, digital scan control, target identification and raid assessment, and will have better electronic counter countermeasures using a low-sidelobe antenna and sidelobe blanking guard channel, frequency agility, and will feature a new high-speed digital signal processor. APG-71 will also have non-co-operative target identification to improve upon current IFF (identification friend or foe).

The first F-14D is expected to enter US Navy service in early 1990 and should allow the fighter to cope with the very much more sophisticated ECM technologies developed since the F-14 first went into production, and counter threats into the 21st century. What form the long-term projected VFMX Tomcat replacement will take is currently unsure, but it can safely be assumed that Tomcat

Right: Production of the McDonnell Douglas F/A-18 Hornet naval strike fighter into the 1990s will guarantee continued service in AD 2000.

Below right: A colony of US Marine Corps Hornets capable of delivering a lethal 'sting.'

Below: Part of a modern US Carrier Battle Group (CBG), with the supercarrier *Nimitz* at its heart. By AD 2000 the Navy will have its planned 15-carrier force. *Nimitz* is expected to remain in service until at least AD 2020.

Right: Pratt & Whitney PW1120 being installed in an IAF F-4 Phantom II. The twin PW1120-engined F-4 made its first flight in 1986.

Left: Hornet's three CRT (Cathode-Ray-Tube) head-down displays are reflected in the pilot's visor.

Below right: F-15E demonstrator armed for a dual role, carrying bombs underwing, underfuselage and tangentially on its conformal fuel tanks.

Below: F/A-18 Hornet demonstrator armed with the new AIM-120A AMRAAM advanced medium-range missile.

will remain the main US Navy air-superiority fighter in AD 2000.

Structurally, Tomcat was a pioneer of composite materials, its tailplane skins of boron epoxy being the first composite production components built for any aircraft. Other primary materials are titanium, aluminum alloy and steel. However, while updates to existing combat aircraft can be made, little can be done to improve upon their basic aerodynamic and structural efficiencies, and this applies to any current aircraft intended to see out the remaining years of this century.

The US Navy's other current fighter is the F/A-18A Hornet, intended actually as a dual strike aircraft and fighter. Joining the US Navy/Marine Corps from 1983 and also being taken into service by the air forces of Australia, Canada and Spain, it is a single-seater powered by two 16,000lb (7257kg) thrust General Electric F404-GE-400 low bypass turbofan engines. It uses a quadruplex digital fly-by-wire flight control system with electrical/mechanical backup. Composite materials are incorporated into its wings and other components, though light alloy is the primary material. Speed is above Mach 1.8 and eventually its main air-to-air missile armament will be AMRAAMs. For strike, Hornet can carry a 17,000lb (7710kg) load, effectively making fighter escort unnecessary as it can set out on a mission with strike weapons prominent and return as a fighter with the remaining air-to-air missiles on board. Production of Hornet will last into the 1990s and keep it in service into the next century. It may well be escorted even in AD 2000 by a fifth generation ADVCAP EA-6 Prowler

The F-16C version of the Fighting Falcon looks similar to the F-16A except for a slightly expanded vertical tail root fairing, but internal updates include enhanced radar for all-weather operations and weapons delivery, an advanced cockpit, and expanded memory/speed/reprogramability of computers. The first F-16C entered service in 1984.

AF
83 118

Left: Artist's impression of an advanced technology STOL Eagle attempting to land on a cratered runway, aided by foreplanes, two-dimensional thrust-vectoring nozzles and a rough/soft field STOL undercarriage. The manufacturer believes only about 1250ft (381m) of runway between craters would be required to land.

tactical jamming aircraft, which will use its ADVanced CAPability (ADVCAP) jamming systems to protect friendly armed aircraft from hostile enemy air-defense systems. The ADVCAP Prowler could be phased into US Navy carrier operations during the 1990s.

By AD 2000 the McDonnell Douglas F-4 Phantom II will no longer be a first-line aircraft, despite current update programs to maintain its capabilities into the 1990s. One such program is being undertaken by IAI (Israel Aircraft Industries) in co-operation with the Israeli Air Force and Pratt & Whitney, which is installing Pratt & Whitney PW1120 engines in place of the original J79s. This gives a thrust-to-weight ratio better than 1, by virtue of a 15-20 percent increase in engine thrust coupled with an approximate 1500lb (680kg) decrease in aircraft weight. Other modifications relate to the avionics and electrical systems. With approximately 2700 F-4s still in service worldwide, Boeing also is offering an improvement program based on the PW1120 and possibly incorporating the installation of the Hornet's APG-65 type multimission radar, a GEC Avionics head-up display and air data computer, Honeywell 423 ring laser gyro inertial navigation system and Sperry multifunction display system.

The USAF's main air superiority fighter is the McDonnell Douglas F-15 Eagle, which first entered service in 1974. It will remain in production into the early 1990s, so guaranteeing its place in AD 2000 despite the development of an ATF (Advanced Tactical Fighter). The current production models are the F-15C single-seater and F-15D two-seater trainer, while earlier F-15As and F-15Bs

began deployment with Air National Guard units in 1985. Eagles are also in service with Japan, Israel and Saudi Arabia.

Eagle is mainly of light alloy and titanium construction, with some use of graphite/epoxy. Its maximum speed of above Mach 2.5 comes from the adoption of two 23,830lb (10,810kg) thrust with afterburning Pratt & Whitney F100-PW-100 turbofans, the nozzles of which are positioned between the twin fins/rudders and the two halves of the all-moving tailplane.

The current Hughes Aircraft APG-63 X-band pulse-Doppler radar is being superseded by the APG-70 under the 1983 multistage improvement program (MSIP), which will provide a 75 percent greater rf bandwidth, a greater lookdown detection range and a significant increase in time between failures. APG-70 is compatible with Eagle's current Sparrow and Sidewinder missile armament and also with AMRAAM when fitted. APG-70 has a very substantial improvement in memory capability compared to the older system and treble the processing speed. Other improvements under MSIP include upgrading of the aircraft's central computer and superseding the Eagle's cockpit control panel for the armament control system with a single multipurpose color video screen.

While the Eagle fighter has a good secondary attack capability, the USAF intends to take into service from 1988 a special long-range interdiction version known as the F-15E. Carrying up to a 23,500lb (10,660kg) weapon load for ground attack or air-to-air missiles in a secondary fighter role (including AMRAAM), it is an all-weather aircraft with the APG-70 radar fitted as standard from the outset. Barring possible cancellation of the program in an effort to divert US defense budget resources to other projects, the USAF could receive just under 400, thereby making it an important type for AD 2000 and before. In addition to the new radar, the F-15E would have wide-field forward-looking infra-red (FLIR) and a LANTIRN navigation/attack pod for target detection and identification and to improve the accuracy of the attack. In the forward cockpit would be three cathode-ray tubes giving displays for navigation (including moving map, radar mapping and terrain following), weapons delivery and systems, plus a wide field of view HUD and redesigned controls for the digital triple-redundant flight control system. Rear cockpit CRT displays would be used for radar weapon selection and recording enemy tracking systems.

An advanced technology version of the Eagle is under consideration which could remain operational even after enemy attacks had cratered runways and greatly reduced the usable runway length. The US Air Force Wright Aeronautical Laboratories and McDonnell Douglas are investigating this possible STOL version. A demonstrator could be flying by 1988 and service deployment could begin in the 1990s. Interestingly, there has been some speculation regarding a similar STOL variant of the Soviet fighter *Foxhound.*

The principal design features of a STOL Eagle would be controllable foreplanes fitted to the air intake trunks (that could operate symmetrically and asymmetrically for pitch and roll moments and help keep the aircraft stable during STOL operations) and carbonfiber vectoring nozzles fitted to the engines. The nozzles, which would be rectangular and two-dimensional, would enable the engine thrust to be vectored by as much as 20 degrees up or down, and thrust reverser vanes would assist in fast deceleration which would be essential to achieve a short landing roll. A digital fly-by-wire system would integrate the functions of all the moving control surfaces and the vectoring nozzles. Maneuvering, especially roll rate, would also benefit from these STOL features, as could payload. McDonnell Douglas believes a STOL Eagle could land and take off in distances of 1250ft (381m) and 1000ft (305m) respectively, compared to the normal landing run without braking parachute of 3500ft (1067m).

The other USAF fighter that will remain prominent in AD 2000 is the General Dynamics F-16 Fighting Falcon, which will also still be in major service with current and future foreign operators. The F-16 joined the USAF in 1979 and, despite being termed a 'lightweight' air combat fighter, can

Below: Advanced flight simulators are used to train pilots and test new aircraft capabilities. Here an F/A-18 pilot sits in a fully integrated cockpit with advanced displays and controls and 'flies' alongside a computer-generated F/A-18. The simulator allows 'live' air and ground scenes.

have a maximum take-off weight of 37,500lb (17,010kg) and achieve a speed of above Mach 2 on the power of its single 25,000lb (11,340kg) thrust Pratt & Whitney F100-PW-200 turbofan engine. Current production F-16C single-seaters and two-seat training F-16Ds have features specified under the F-16 Multinational Staged Improvement Program (MSIP) to enhance aircraft capabilities for beyond-visual-range interception, precision strike and night attack roles. These model F-16s (and those modified) can carry AMRAAM and other advanced missiles and will be fitted with the LANTIRN nav/attack and ASPJ jamming systems. An adversary aircraft version of the F-16 to be used by the US Navy for training is designated F-16N, while a reconnaissance version to supersede RF-4Cs with the USAF is known as the F-16G.

The F-16 is an advanced design, which introduced many new features to squadron pilots. It has a blended wing and fuselage. This design innovation increases the amount of fuel carried internally and also means that the fuselage provides lift at high angles of attack. Most of the airframe is of metal construction, though the tail fin and all-moving tailplane have composite material skins. It

Above: The F-16 MSIP gives the Fighting Falcon the capability to carry beyond-visual-range missiles for interception and improvements for precision-strike and night-attack missions. In addition to two wingtip Sidewinders, this F-16 has four AIM-120A AMRAAMs.

Left: Pilot's eye view of the F-16C/D cockpit, featuring in the top center the GEC Avionics wide-angle electronic head-up display.

Above right: Two F-1 6XL advanced technology Fighting Falcons showing their compound sweep 'cranked arrow' wings, both carrying AMRAAM missiles semisubmerged at the wing/fuselage intersection and one with twelve 500lb bombs. With the bombload, the F-16XL has shown its capability to roll while keeping a 30° angle of attack at 104mph (167km/h).

Right: F-1 6XL engaged in air-to-air refueling.

uses a quadruple-redundant fly-by-wire control system, thus allowing the aircraft's center of gravity to be moved aft in typical CCV (control configured vehicle) relaxed static stability style, greatly reducing trim drag at high load factors and supersonic speeds and enhancing maneuverability. The latest radar is the Westinghouse APG-68 pulse-Doppler range and angle track unit, necessary for improved all-weather capabilities, the launch of beyond-visual-range missiles, and to improve ground-mapping performance. In track-while-scan mode, the radar can track 10 targets simultaneously, assess each threat and launch missiles.

A more advanced development of the F-16 is the F-16XL, a company-funded combat aircraft that will enter production in 1991 as a dual-role fighter and attack aircraft under the USAF designation F-16F. The most obvious change is the adoption of the 'cranked arrow' wing with 50 and 70 degrees of compound leading-edge sweepback. The wing is blended into the lengthened fuselage, which carries more internal fuel, and removes the need for a tailplane. Wing area of the XL is a remarkable 663sq ft (61.6m^2) compared to the standard F-16's 300sq ft (27.87m^2), though offering reduced drag at the best cruising speed. Graphite/bismaleimide composite skins are used on the wings to allow improved aeroelastic deformed shapes under load and offer high strength with low weight. The increased fuel load, improved cruise flight efficiency and lower weapons drag achieved by carrying AMRAAM missiles in semi-submerged state (returning nearer to the F-106 concept of internally housed missiles, but without the structural complications of a bay) improves combat radius by nearly half as much again. The maximum weapon load for attack is increased from 12,000lb (5443kg) for the standard F-16 to 15,000lb (6800kg), and penetration speed in the attack role without the use of the fuel-guzzling afterburner is higher.

Alongside development of advanced versions and derivatives of existing fighters to serve out what remains of the 20th century and hold the fort until the next generation of superfighters is prepared for service, plans for the future have begun. One such program is known as ATF (Advanced Tactical Fighter) and will eventually produce at least one combat aircraft type combining most of the advanced technologies previously discussed, enabling it to perform well in the twenty-first century as an Eagle replacement.

Required to be available by the mid 1990s, ATF is likely to be strange in configuration to today's eyes. High speed will remain important to the ATF, but this will mean the ability to cruise supersonically and not just possess supersonic 'dash' capability for short periods like today's combat aircraft. Supersonic cruising at high altitudes will allow more rapid engagement of the enemy and make the task of enemy surface-to-air missiles more difficult. As remarked by Grumman Aerospace – one of seven US companies involved in ATF (the others being Boeing, General Dynamics, Lockheed, McDonnell Douglas, Northrop and Rockwell International) – 'such capabilities mean the fighter can enter an air battle in a high total energy state,

tradable for altitude or maneuverability as the combat situation demands.'

The ATF will need to be successful at all speeds, remaining fully controllable even at low subsonic speeds and at high angles of attack, since an air battle often (in the words of Grumman) 'starts high and fast, but after a few minutes it usually winds up low and slow.' High maneuverability will be a

Above: There are many conceptions for a possible US Advanced Tactical Fighter (ATF), a representation of which are included in this book. This Lockheed-California artist's conception has maneuverability, low-observables and supersonic cruising as its keynotes, enabling the ATF to engage enemy fighters over their own territory. Short take-off and landing capability would allow it to use airfields with combat damage, while high reliability and low maintenance would permit use of airfields with minimum support facilities.

Left: An ATF configuration optimized for moderate Mach supersonic cruise flight, having highly-swept double delta wings and twin tail-mounted engines. The long fuselage would give plenty of scope for large internal fuel tanks, avionics and even a bay for the air-to-air missiles, while the wings have trailing-edge and leading-edge maneuvering flaps.

Above: Another Grumman ATF design has highly-swept wings and moving foreplanes, with two-dimensional (2D) vectoring nozzles for the engines buried in the wing roots.

Right: One of Rockwell International's North American Aircraft Operations' (NAAO) conceptual designs for a 1990s fighter, this proposal clearly takes notice of low observable technology but, perhaps surprisingly, has outward-canted fins. More than 60ft (18.3m) in length, it has two-dimensional vectoring nozzles and carries four medium-range (AMRAAM) and two short-range (ASRAAM) missiles semisubmerged under the wide blended fuselage between the engines, with further missiles carried under the outer wing panels and at the wingtips. Cannon still will be carried by the 1990s fighter, as shown by the port trough in the fuselage ahead of the wing.

requirement of ATF, achieved not only through airframe design but the evolution of vectored thrust versions of the turbofan engines, power plants that will offer thrust-to-weight ratio im-

provements of perhaps 25 percent compared to existing engines through lighter weight due to a rethink of the compressor and turbine design. Engine bypass ratio for ATF engines will be neces-

Left: This Boeing ATF benefits from powered moving foreplanes, two-dimensional vectoring nozzles to the engines for short take-off/landing and maneuvering, and semisubmerged missiles.

Below: This Grumman X-29A-style ATF has design emphasis on supersonic performance combined with high maneuverability.

Right: A McDonnell Douglas conceptual model of an ATF, configured for cruising at supersonic speeds.

Below right: Another McDonnell Douglas impression of an ATF, this time with 'straight' rear wings and foreplanes.

sarily lower than today to allow long duration supersonic cruising without resorting to afterburners. As already mentioned for Eagle, thrust vectoring will also enable the ATF to overcome badly damaged runways, though such an aircraft would also be required to operate from rough, temporary strips.

ATF will have an advanced cockpit layout with multifunction displays and so on, but it will also be hardened against wartime nuclear, chemical and biological warfare environments, providing the pilot with 'clean' air. The pilot himself will be required to wear a special protective flying suit in case of damage to the aircraft or an emergency escape. The ATF's avionics will also have to be of sufficient complexity to enable it to complete its missions with or without the assistance of AWACS type aircraft and navigational Global Positioning Satellites, both of which would be prime targets in the event of war.

Another major factor in the ATF design will be the emergence of an ultra-reliable radar, which will also be used to update the B-1B bomber and the F-15 and F-16 fighters. Current combat aircraft radars often have only 40 or 50 hours between

Above: High supersonic cruise would be a feature of this ATF, its advanced turbofan engines carried in the broad fuselage and fed with air via side intakes with semicircular centerbodies and exhausting through two-dimensional vectoring nozzles with infrared shielding. Other features are close-coupled variable camber wings and foreplanes, advanced ECM in wingtip pods, and conformal weapons carriage.

failures, thereby greatly reducing the number of aircraft serviceable at any one time. The URR program is expected to produce a radar capable of 10 times this reliability, incorporating an active element phased-array antenna with about 2000 individual power-handling modules (some of which can fail without making it inoperable). High-speed computing might be used, allowing a possible 100 times improvement in data throughput coupled with reduced size and weight. Development of the URR will certainly continue into the 1990s.

In the meantime, while the world has to wait for ATF type superfighters, non-superpower nations are getting on with the job of pressing advanced designs into service. Many have already been mentioned, but one that has not is Lavi. Like most modern combat aircraft, but especially because it is intended to supersede the Israeli Air Force's current IAI Kfir-C2 and -C7 strike-fighters and Douglas A-4 Skyhawk light attack aircraft, Lavi has been designed for many roles including close air support, interdiction and secondary air defense. Developed by Israel Aircraft Industries, it is a single-seater in combat form with close-coupled swept-delta rear wings and all-moving swept-delta foreplanes, 22 percent of its structural weight comprising composite materials. Grumman Aerospace assisted in the design, development and early production of the wings and fins, owing to their advanced substructure and skins of carbon-

fiber composite construction. Power is provided by a 20,680lb (9380kg) thrust with afterburning Pratt & Whitney PW1120 engine, bestowing a maximum speed of Mach 1.85. Advanced avionics and systems include a quadruple-redundant digital fly-by-wire control system with no mechanical back-up, a wide angle holographic HUD and three multifunction cockpit displays, the cockpit typically designed to minimize pilot workload and allow full hands on throttle and stick (HOTAS) operation. The Elta multimode pulse-Doppler radar has automatic target acquisition and track-while-scan modes for air defense and beam-sharpened ground mapping, terrain avoidance and sea search modes for air-to-ground combat and surveillance missions.

As a sensor of the weapon system, the radar determines both airborne and ground target data, such as position, velocity and acceleration. Its coherent transmitter and stable multichannel receiver gives lookdown performance over a broad band of frequencies as well as accurate resolution for mapping.

Lavi's configuration provides vortex lift at high angles of attack, giving exceptional turn performance and handling qualities, with control achieved by nine independently commanded surfaces. The prototype Lavi flew for the first time in 1986 and initial operational deployment will begin in about 1992. At least 300 Lavis are expected to be built by the Israelis.

Above: IAI Lavi mockup with a PW1120 engine to the rear.

Right: Kfir-C7 multimission fighters on air defense duty, each carrying four Shafrir air-to-air missiles and drop tank.

Above: Agusta A129 Mangusta attack helicopter for Italian Army service from 1987.

Left: The AH-1T+ SuperCobra. Sidewinder air-to-air missiles are among its weapon options.

Below: Artist's impression of Mi-28 *Havoc*.

Soon to join the airplanes mentioned in this chapter, and the possible spacefighter detailed in chapter one, is a new breed of fighter – the fighter helicopter. The world's current attack helicopters – such as the tandem two-seat Italian Agusta A129 Mangusta, the Soviet Mil Mi-24 *Hind-E* and nose-mounted radar equipped Mi-28 *Havoc* (due to become operational later this decade), the US Bell HueyCobra and McDonnell Douglas AH-64A Apache – all have air-to-air capability with guns and short-range missiles for anti-helicopter duties

Above: The first fully comprehensive artist's impression of the new Soviet Kamov *Hokum*, which is already flying and some believe is at least as good as the US Army's as yet not built LHX in a helicopter air-superiority role.

Left: US Army Apache, making use of natural cover to hide its intention of a surprise attack.

Top right: One of the McDonnell Douglas Helicopters' conceptions for a US Army LHX helicopter in combat form, with a NOTAR (No-Tail-Rotor) antitorque system in which pressurized air is vented from the tail which, when pushed downward by the main rotor downwash, follows the contours of the tailcone to produce a side force.

Right: Proposed version of the McDonnell Douglas AH-64A Apache for the US Marine Corps; weaponry including two Sidewinder air-to-air missiles.

in addition to their more usual attack roles. However, the first helicopters designed from the outset with helicopter air-superiority missions in mind (though not exclusively) are now appearing.

The Soviet Union has taken a lead in this field with its armored Kamov *Hokum* (NATO name), which began flight trials in 1984. Typically a Kamov in having coaxial contra-rotating rotors, it is thought to have side-by-side seating for the crew of two and to carry infra-red suppressors and decoy dispensers to enhance survivability in the battle zone. It is thought to possess a maximum speed of 217mph (350km/h) and weapons will no doubt include a heavy caliber gun and tube-launched missiles.

The US project to develop a helicopter fighter is one aspect of the LHX (Light Helicopter Experimental) program, in which a family of related light scout/attack and utility helicopters is envisaged to replace the Bell Iroquois utility, AH-1 HueyCobra attack, OH-58 Kiowa observation and OH-6A Cayuse helicopters in US Army service. The LHX program could cover over 5000 new helicopters and five industry teams are presently competing for contracts.

To enter service from the 1990s and to fulfill part of the US Army's AirLand Battle 2000 plan – in which an enemy's numerically superior forces can be defeated by highly mobile action, surprise, deception and outmaneuvering to exploit its inability to respond quickly enough – the combat elements of LHX would be expected to engage in actual helicopter air-to-air fighting. Therefore a battlefield of the early 21st century could see UH-60 Black Hawk and LHX utility helicopters supported by Apaches and LHX combat types.

Despite the variety of tasks required of the LHX helicopters, they are expected to have commonality of engines, rotors and other dynamic components, to be capable of all-weather, day and night nap-of-the-earth operations, to be autonomous in operation if required, and have such advanced features as composite airframes, low-observable technology, digital avionics and flight controls, simplified cockpit arrangement to permit single pilot operation, and conformal carriage of ordnance to reduce drag.

Above: Boeing Vertol and Sikorsky teamed for the LHX program in June 1985. Before this Boeing had produced its own LHX concept able to perform the required single pilot scout, attack and utility missions at night and in adverse weather. Seen here in the scout/attack role, the mast-mounted sight has located two enemy targets which are being attacked under computer control by missile and cannon. Flares ejected from under the helicopter's fuselage offer self-protection against a retaliatory attack. The helicopter has an automated cockpit with computer augmented imagery and voice actuated controls.

Left: Another Boeing Vertol conception of an LHX helicopter in SCAT role, this time with the pilot having normal outside vision.

Right: Bell is now pinning its hopes for the LHX program on the required 'conventional' helicopter, incorporating a bearingless main rotor, composite materials, twin 1200shp turboshaft engines and a ring-fan tail rotor. In SCAT form it will carry Hellfire antitank and Stinger antiaircraft missiles, rockets and cannon and will be capable of 'hands off' operation while automatically seeking, identifying and assessing priority targets.

At present the primary mission weight for LHX is set at 7500-8500lb (3400-3855kg) and speed at 190mph (315km/h), the armed LHX carrying Hellfire antiarmor and Stinger antiaircraft missiles. Artist's impressions of some of these projected LHX contenders are shown and their design features detailed in the captions.

Above: When the US Army announced that it was looking for a conventional helicopter rather than a tiltrotor type to fulfil its LHX program, it effectively put an end to what might have been the most promising configuration, especially in terms of speed. A tilt-rotor type might have been capable of 350mph (563km/h),

with its large rotors turning upward for vertical flight and hovering and turned forward for horizontal cruising.

Left: Bell Helicopter Textron has the greatest experience with tilt-rotor design, its XV-15 research aircraft having flown successfully since 1977.

Below: A Sikorsky conception of 1984 shows an X-wing holicoptor with a rotor of about 50ft (15.25m) and a vectored-thrust antitorque system. Envisaged as a possible Viking, Prowler or Hawkeye replacement for around AD 2000, the main rotor would be stopped at about the normal maximum speed for combat helicopters, thereafter acting as a fixed wing to permit speeds possibly in excess of 500mph (800km/h).

Above: Phalanx MP-15 Dragon depicted on an antihelicopter mission.

Opposite: A slightly less ambitious X-wing helicopter from Sikorsky, this would be capable of about 318mph (512km/h) on the power of two 2500shp engines with variable-pitch fans mounted on the fuselage sides.

Helicopters may also be potential replacements for some fixed-wing aircraft currently serving on board US Navy aircraft carriers. Sikorsky, for one, has looked at the X-wing helicopter, in which the rotor is stopped during cruising flight to allow the blades to function as fixed wings. Such a helicopter is said to be a possible suitable replacement for the Lockheed Viking antisubmarine, the Prowler ECM and E-2C Hawkeye early-warning aircraft, with the potential of high speed and V/STOL. However, even looking to the future this seems unlikely, though the X-wing helicopter might find an application. What is certain is that the greater the combat potential of the helicopter, the more urgent becomes the countermeasure. Air superiority helicopters may be one answer, but another is fixed-wing aircraft configured for an antihelicopter role. This, in fact, is one of 36 specified roles for the projected American Phalanx MP-18 Dragon. The Dragon is unorthodox in design, able to use different modules and rear fuselage sections to suit the wide variety of missions. It has been designed to incorporate stealth technology, will be constructed of composite materials and will use two small turbofan engines with two pairs of three-dimensional vectoring nozzles to achieve VTOL operation. The estimated maximum speed of Mach 2.5 would be achieved by the adoption of a very lightweight low drag design, with a take-off weight of only about 5800lb (2630kg) in two-seat armed form. Prototypes were reportedly under construction in 1985. Naturally, for antihelicopter use the Dragon would need to be low subsonic.

Fighters of AD 2000 will take many forms. Aircraft familiar to our present skies will be joined by spectacular warplanes of design still to be frozen, and helicopters will stalk their own airborne prey.

6· TWENTY-FIRST CENTURY BOMBERS

To detail bombers of AD 2000 takes surprisingly little space. Firstly, only those bombers known to be in existence today, either being built and deployed or under development, will be in service at the turn of the century. Secondly, few nations will retain bombers (as opposed to attack aircraft) by that date. The RAF, for example, once boasted an impressive bomber force but now its remaining V-bombers have been converted into flight refueling tankers. France may well rely only on its two-seat, low-altitude Mirage 2000N to undertake penetration attacks with nuclear missiles by the later 1990s, having seen the last of its remaining Mirage IV-Ps pass out of service during that decade.

China is really the unknown quantity, in the 1980s seemingly content to rely mainly on updated and upgraded variants of 1950s-technology warplanes of mostly Soviet origin. China is almost certain to have superseded its present fighters and Nanchang Q-5-type attack aircraft by the 1990s, including the indigenous Shenyang J-8 Mach 2.3 single-seat fighter. More urgent will be the replacement of its fleet of H-5 (Ilyushin Il-28), H-6 (Tupolev Tu-16) and Tupolev Tu-4 (Boeing Superfortress type) bombers if it is to maintain its airborne nuclear deterrent. Such a bomber is within the growing capabilities of China to develop,

though the strength of such an aircraft would probably be drawn as much from numbers as from high technology.

This leaves the superpowers of the Soviet Union and USA to continue with bombers in the conventional way, drawing upon the latest technologies in materials, avionics, power plant and design to cloak them from the ever more sophisticated defense and sensing systems. The Soviet Union has persistently been the most logical in its postwar development of bombers, using all the resources at hand and providing the necessary budgets to maintain an offensive force at the forefront of modern technology.

The Soviet Union currently has three bombers in production, two of which are in service now and the third to join the forces around 1988. All of these will still be in service in AD 2000, well before which date the Tupolev Tu-16 *Badger*, most versions of the Tupolev Tu-95/-142 *Bear*, Tupolev Tu-22 *Blinder* and Myasishchev M-4 *Bison* will have been withdrawn.

The most surprising of the AD 2000 bombers will be the remaining *Bear-Hs*, examples of the latest production version of the Tupolev Tu-95/-142 strategic bomber and maritime aircraft that has its pedigree stretching back to the original *Bears* observed at the Soviet Aviation Day display at

Previous pages: Dassault Mirage IV-P bomber carrying an ASMP nuclear missile, making a rocket-assisted take-off.

Below: US Department of Defense drawing of a Soviet Tupolev *Bear-H* bomber launching an AS-15 cruise missile.

Tushino in 1955. Of course *Bear-H* is greatly more sophisticated than the early bombers but the overall configuration remains the same, with huge 167ft 8in (51.10m) span wings swept at 37 degrees, a long circular-section conventional fuselage, and power provided by four of the world's most powerful turboprop engines (14,795ehp Kuznetsov NK-12MVs, each driving two contra-rotating propellers). Yes, a propeller-driven bomber will still be around in AD 2000!

Bear-H was put into production as the carrier aircraft for long-range cruise missiles, such as the present 1850 mile (3000km) range AS-15 with nuclear warhead. These give units new theater stand-off and strategic attack capability. Though slow by later bomber standards, probably with an over-target speed of 575mph (925km/h), *Bear-H* has the benefit of extremely long range, again estimated at about 7800 miles (12,550km) with in-flight refueling. *Bear-H* became operational in Soviet forces in 1984.

A bomber with no Western equivalent is the Soviet Tu-26 *Backfire*, a logical successor to the fairly unsuccessful Tu-22, which joined both the Air Force and Naval Aviation from the mid 1970s. Several hundred were operational by the mid 1980s (with production continuing), being assigned strategic and theater nuclear and conventional attack, antishipping and reconnaissance roles. While easily capable of reaching the USA on a high-altitude subsonic mission, using in-flight refueling, *Backfire* is at its element over Europe and the Atlantic, undertaking perhaps low-level penetration attacks with supersonic dash.

Of metal construction, *Backfire* has a fixed center section to its wings and variable-geometry outer sections which can be swept to approximately 65 degrees. With wings spread, the sweep-back angle is about 20 degrees. Probably carrying a crew of four, it achieves its approximate Mach 1.92 high-altitude speed with power from two large afterburning turbofan engines, reportedly derived from the 44,092lb (20,000kg) thrust Kuznetsov NK-144. Low altitude speed is only just below Mach 1. Current *Backfires* carry *Kitchen* or *Kingfish* air-to-surface nuclear or high-explosive missiles or bombs, and survivability is improved by the use of decoy missiles and extremely advanced ECM/ECCM. But even these measures, meant to help it penetrate the most advanced defense systems, will not enable it to maintain a penetration role past the mid 1990s, when it will almost certainly carry newly developed missiles.

Strategic penetration roles will be taken over by the new Tupolev *Blackjack* bomber, which represents the expected high supersonic replacement

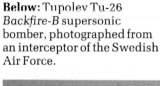

Below: Tupolev Tu-26 *Backfire-B* supersonic bomber, photographed from an interceptor of the Swedish Air Force.

Above: US Department of Defense impression of the latest Soviet strategic bomber known as *Blackjack*.

Left: AS-4 *Kitchen* supersonic high-explosive or nuclear stand-off missile under the fuselage of a *Backfire-B* bomber.

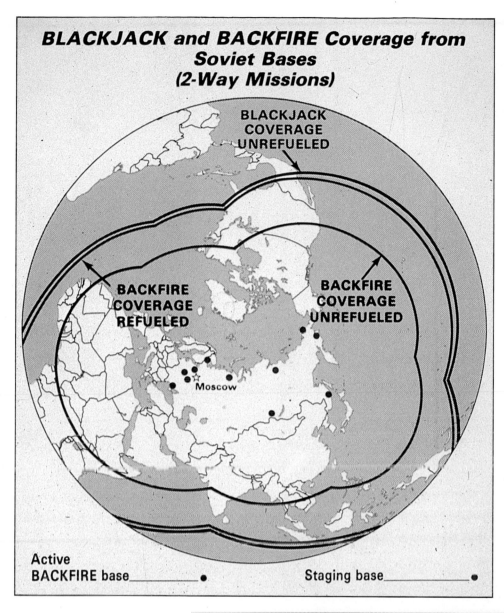

BLACKJACK and BACKFIRE Coverage from Soviet Bases (2-Way Missions)

BLACKJACK COVERAGE UNREFUELED

BACKFIRE COVERAGE REFUELED

BACKFIRE COVERAGE UNREFUELED

Moscow

Active BACKFIRE base ● Staging base ●

for *Bison* and *Bear*. It will join Soviet units from 1988. This most formidable strategic bomber is basically a cruise missile carrier, but retains the capability to carry other types of missile and bombs. It was first 'seen' in a satellite photograph taken on 25 November 1981 while undergoing trials at the Ramenskoye flight test center.

Blackjack will take the Soviet strategic bomber force into the 21st century, though even this bomber will be superseded in the penetration role before then. Like *Backfire* it has variable-geometry outer wing panels but in most other respects it is quite different. With a spread wing span estimated at 172ft (52m), it achieves its believed high-altitude performance of Mach 2+ by the adoption of four large and powerful turbojets, possibly Koliesovs in the 44,092lb (20,000kg) thrust range. Unrefueled radius of action is said to be about 4535 miles (7300km). Some 100 are likely to be built.

The latest Soviet bomber in AD 2000 will undoubtedly be a stealth type, though of course *Blackjack* was designed to incorporate many of the same kinds of 'low-observable' technologies to be found on the USAF's B-1B. What form this will take is uncertain, but it is true to say that any technology pursued in the West will have a Soviet equivalent if it has any chance of success. This new bomber would take over the penetration role from the later 1990s, degrading *Blackjack* to undertaking missions on the periphery of an enemy's defense systems.

With the Boeing B-52 Stratofortress expected to be retired from all major roles by the turn of the century and the General Dynamics FB-111A also outdated, the United States Air Force is likely to have only two bombers in service by AD 2000. The 100 Rockwell International B-1Bs that have already begun entering squadron service will be

Above: US Department of Defense map said to show the unrefueled and refueled radius of action for *Backfire* and unrefueled radius of *Blackjack*.

Right: B-1B with wings spread. This bomber offers a radar signature 100 times smaller than that of the B-52 due to the use of low observable technology.

Above: The B-1B's General Electric turbofan engines are carried in pairs beneath the fixed portion of the wings and have fixed-geometry inlets.

joined by examples of the Northrop ATB (Advanced Technology Bomber). Small tactical aircraft may also be called upon to undertake bombing missions, relying on super long-range and very advanced stealth-type cruise missiles to fly the long distances between launching position and target, and overcome enemy over-the-horizon radars and other defense systems. Such stealth cruise missiles would probably be carried conformally against the airframe of the launch aircraft, each missile carrying a nuclear or conventional warhead or even submunitions to destroy many targets in one swoop. Such missiles could be programed to avoid known enemy defense systems and use their 'thinking' capability to assess situations and complete autonomous attacks. Both the Soviet Union and the USA are engaged in such research, the US projected system being known currently as AWCIT (Advanced Weapon Carriage Integration Technology).

The availability of strategic ballistic missiles launched from land silos and submarines, coupled with the sophistication of air defenses, went a long way in sounding the death knoll of the strategic

bomber for many air forces. However, the superpowers have worked on the basis of triad strategic forces, encompassing airborne, land-based and sea missile systems. Unlike the Soviet Union, the USA allowed its bomber force to remain largely unaffected by the possibilities of producing more advanced designs than its early generation heavy long-range jet type, its incredible North American B-70 Valkyrie Mach 3 cruise bomber of 1964 first flight and the original B-1 being cancelled before production. This left the B-52 as the only triad heavy bomber element, but with continuous updating and modifications to improve avionics and weaponry.

In 1985, however, the first production Rockwell International B-1B long-range multirole strategic bomber appeared, and this type will take over strategic penetration missions until itself superseded in the later 1990s by the ATB, after which time it will undertake less hazardous missions. The B-1B is a 136ft 8in (41.67m) span (spread) variable-geometry bomber, capable of a maximum speed of Mach 1.25 on the power from its four 30,000lb (13,610kg) thrust General Electric F101-

GE-102 augmented turbofan engines (carried in pairs beneath the fixed-wing center section). At a low level penetration altitude of about 200ft (61m), speed is over 600mph (965km/h), and the range without in-flight refueling is an impressive 7455 miles (12,000km). A crew of four is standard, and weapons can include up to 22 air-launched cruise missiles or other missiles or bombs carried internally and externally. In a conventional bombing role, a typical load would be 64,000lb (29,030kg) of high-explosive bombs.

As for the Soviet variable-geometry bombers, swing-wings in spread position allow the B-1B to take off in shorter distances than would otherwise be possible, enabling it to clear airfields quickly if under the threat of attack and use shorter runways if its home base has been destroyed. With the wings swept, it takes on the ideal configuration for high subsonic or supersonic flight.

Though mainly of metal construction (aluminum alloys and titanium), the B-1B incorporates considerable 'low-observable' technology to enable it to defeat enemy defense systems. It has a blended airframe that gives a radar signature 100 times smaller than that of the B-52 (see chapter 2) and very advanced avionics. Offensive avionics include the AN/APQ-164 radar system, which has

a low-observable phased array antenna for low altitude terrain following and terrain avoidance and for navigation. Other functions include weapon delivery. The B-1B has a very accurate inertial navigation system and can use the Air Force Satellite Communications system (AFSAT-COM). In order to make the B-1B survivable in a dense enemy radar environment, the bomber uses the AN/ALQ-161 ECM system to jam enemy signals and also receive new enemy signals in order to compute the updated threat and jam accordingly. Chaff and flares are among other defensive measures.

As previously mentioned, Northrop is developing the follow-up bomber to the B-1B, about which little is known owing to intense secrecy surrounding the project. It has been reported that contracts worth $7,300,000,000 have already been awarded to the company, which is receiving assistance from several US aerospace companies including Boeing, LTV and General Electric. A mock-up of the ATB (Advanced Technology Bomber) has been built and the first prototype is expected to fly in November 1987. Operational deployment could begin in the mid 1990s.

The ATB will be a true stealth bomber in every sense. If of very advanced delta form it could be

Below: What the Northrop ATB (Advanced Technology Bomber) looks like is an official secret. It may prove to be a flying wing design, similar in conception to the illustrated YB-49 but much more modern, smaller and using low observable technology to give it a radar cross-section of possibly only one-thousandth that of a B-52 Stratofortress.

smaller than the B-1B, powered by perhaps two non-afterburning turbofan engines for long range, probably subsonic in cruise, and possessing low infra-red signature. More likely, however, is a 'flying wing' configuration, in which no conventional tail unit or fuselage is used and the engines, crew and so on are all accommodated within the contours of the aerofoil. This configuration has several advantages. Not only can the entire airframe contribute to 'lift,' but it removes such radar reflective surfaces as tailfins from the structure and thereby maintains the best possible stealth blended airframe configuration.

Flying wing bombers are not new to Northrop, which built and flew prototype and pre-production piston and turbojet powered bombers during the later 1940s under the YB-35 and YB-49 designations respectively. Such was their success that even a commercial airliner flying wing was projected, but in the event the more conventional B-36 Peacemaker bomber was chosen for service in the YB-49's place.

The ATB could well be the last US bomber to fly conventionally, as many experts believe the way forward to be the Trans-Atmospheric Vehicle (TAV). This would be an advanced shuttle-like aircraft, air-launched in the atmosphere, or would take off from a jettisonable powered trolley to go into low orbit before sweeping down to target and eventually making a conventional landing on a runway at low speed. This would permit very high speeds to be achieved, perhaps as high as the upper Mach 20s, while allowing a 'loiter' time if required for a mission. Research into this type of vehicle is being undertaken in the USA and USSR, and in Britain British Aerospace's HOTOL has similar capabilities but is probably considered a transport concept. However, TAVs are strategic bombing vehicles for perhaps the mid 21st century.

Other speculations for the future include nuclear-powered aircraft, which could serve as long-endurance cruise missile carriers using the reactors only for cruise flight and conventional engines for take-off and landing. Future anti-submarine aircraft could include large sea control amphibians of perhaps 640,000lb (290,300kg) gross weight and capable of flying over ranges of 3600 miles (5800km). Such naval ASW aircraft could make frequent 'sits' in sea state 5 conditions to prolong the ASW search and use hydroskis during alighting and takeoff. But again this is only speculation and will not come about in the forseeable future though such 'sea loiter' vehicles are not far removed from Soviet *ekranoplan* aircraft. *Ekranoplans* have been tested to make use of the power-augmented ram wing in ground effect (PAR-

Below: Artist's conception of a nuclear-powered aircraft for military use.

Above: Large sea loiter amphibian of some 640,000lb (290,300kg) gross weight, able to carry a 112,400lb (51,000kg) payload of weapons and avionics for sea-control missions. It could fly 3600 miles (5800km), make five 10-hour 'sits' on the water and undertake protracted submarine searches and attacks.

WIG) principle, in which a specially designed flying-boat skims over the sea at a height equal to less than half its wing span. This produces a dynamic cushion of trapped air below the aircraft, enabling a drag reduction of up to, say, 70 percent, and thus gives extremely long range. Such aircraft can fly conventionally, but in surface effect they can combine the best attributes of a fast transport aircraft and naval vessel (in terms of range and better than average load-carrying capability), making them ideal for troop reinforcement and anti-shipping duties, among other roles of which they are capable.

In terms of conventional bombing and attack at sea, the US Navy will stay with its low-level, all-weather and day-and-night Intruder, a 644mph (1037km/h) two-seater, for carrier operations. This will be in A-6F form by the 1990s with 10,700lb (4853kg) thrust General Electric F404-GE-400D non-afterburning turbofan engines and new modern avionics. It will possess the ability to launch advanced missiles. The US Navy is conducting studies for an Intruder replacement under the project name Advanced Combat Aircraft (ACA), but this work is preliminary and few details are yet available.

In many respects the future of the bomber is a little easier to predict than that of the fighter. The currently deployed bombers will soon be joined by squadrons of B-1Bs and *Blackjacks*, and by the 1990s even these variable-geometry types will have to take the background as the 'super-stealth' types become available. In the longer term, Trans-Atmospheric Vehicles are likely to be the bombers of the mid 21st century, so long as in the meantime mankind is sensible enough to keep the bombers at their bases for deterrent purposes and not use them offensively!

INDEX

ACKNOWLEDGMENTS

The author and publisher would like to thank Martin Bristow the designer, Ron Watson for preparing the index and the following individuals and organizations for the use of their pictures:

Aeritalia/Aermacchi/EMBRAER pages 63 (bottom), 66-7
Agusta page 107 (top)
Airship Industries page 24
ALR pages 72 (all 3), 73 (top)
Avions Marcel Dassault-Breguet Aviation pages 17 (top), 44-5 (top), 64 (top), 65 (both), 68, 69 (both), 116-7
Bell Helicopters Textron pages 106, 111, 112, 113, (top)
Boeing Company page 11 (bottom)
Boeing Vertol page 110 (both)
British Aerospace Group pages 4-5, 8-9, 14 (top), 20, 40, 41 (bottom), 42, 50, 51 (bottom), 53, 55, 56, 57, 58, 59, 60-1, 62 (both), 63 (top), 74, 75 (top), 76-7, 78 (center), 81 (top)
Ferranti pages 51 (top), 73 (bottom)
Ford Aerospace & Communications page 91 (top)
GEC Avionics pages 39, 41 (top), 49, 98 (bottom)
General Dynamics pages 48, 80 (bottom), 94-5, 98 (top), 99 (both)
Grumman Aerospace Corporation, Bethpage, pages 2-3, 18-19, 22-3, 26-7, 28, 30-1, 32-3, 34-5, 88 (bottom), 100 (bottom), 101 (top), 102 (bottom), 104
Herkenning Netherlands page 108 (top)
Hughes Aircraft pages 70 (bottom), 89

Israel Aircraft Industries pages 36-7, 38, 93 (top), 105 (both)
Lockheed California, pages 10, 29
Lockheed, Georgia, pages 124, 125
Loral Corporation page 25 (bottom)
Marconi Avionics page 54
McDonnell Douglas pages 43, 78 (top), 79 (top), 80 (top), 82-3, 91 (bottom), 92 (both), 93 (bottom), 96, 97, 103 (both), 108 (bottom), 109 (both)
Ministry of Defense/Cpt Rick Wolfendon page 21
NASA pages 15, 52
Northrop Corporation page 123
Phalanx Organization page 114 (top left)
Rockwell International pages 46-7 (both), 101, 121 (bottom), 122
Rolls-Royce pages 6, 75 (bottom), 79 (bottom)
Royal Navy page 84
Saab-Scania pages 70 (top), 71
Sikorsky Aircraft pages 113 (bottom), 114
Eric Simonsen pages 1, 81 (bottom)
Swedish Airforce page 119
TCOM Corporation page 25 (top)
US Air Force pages 12 (top), 102 (top)
US Air Force/Lockheed California pages 100 (top)
US Department of Defense, pages 11 (top), 12 (bottom), 13, 14 (bottom), 16, 17 (bottom), 85 (both), 86, 87 (all 3), 88 (top), 107 (bottom), 118, 120 (both), 121 (top)
US Navy, page 90